European Business Law and Practice Series

Corporate Acquisitions and Mergers in France

A Practical Guide to the Legal, Financial and Administrative Implications

Other Titles in the Series

Concentration Control in the European Economic Community, P.V.F. Bos, J. Stuyck, P. Wytinck
(ISBN 1-85333-570-3)

European Community Telecommunications Regulation, S. Mosteshar
(ISBN 1-85333-756-0)

Harmonization and Hazard: Regulating Workplace Health and Safety in the European Community, R. Baldwin, T. Daintith (eds.)
(ISBN 1-85333-723-4)

Intellectual Property and the Internal Market of the European Community, P. Groves, A. Martino, C. Miskin, J. Richards
(ISBN 1-85333-575-4)

Privatization in Central and Eastern Europe, P. Šarčević (ed.)
(ISBN 1-85333-713-7)

Corporate Acquisitions & Mergers in Portugal, Ronald Charles Wolf
(ISBN 1-85333-793-5)

European Community and International Media Law, David B. Winn
(ISBN 1-85333-760-9)

Mergers and Joint Ventures in Europe (2nd ed.), Frank L. Fine
(ISBN 1-85333-574-6)

(*Please order by title or ISBN*)

European Business Law and Practice Series

Corporate Acquisitions and Mergers in France

A Practical Guide to the Legal, Financial and Administrative Implications

Charles-Henri de Pardieu
and
Nathalie Weyd

De Pardieu Brocas et Associés

Graham & Trotman
A member of Wolters Kluwer Academic Publishers
LONDON/DORDRECHT/BOSTON

Graham & Trotman Limited
Sterling House
66 Wilton Road
London SW1V 1DE
UK

Kluwer Academic Publishers Group
101 Philip Drive
Assinippi Park
Norwell, MA 02061
USA

ISBN 1 85333 965 2
Series ISBN 1 85333 714 5

First published 1994

British Library Cataloguing in Publication Data

A catalogue record for this book is available from the British Library

Library of Congress CIP data is available

Typeset by Tradespools Ltd, Frome, Somerset
Printed and bound in Great Britain by Athenaeum Press Ltd.,
Newcastle-upon-Tyne

Contents

Preface

This book addresses the legal and tax principles applicable to acquisitions in France, whether the acquisitions are made by means of purchase of assets or shares in public or private companies or by means of merger. It also identifies the critical issues which are often encountered by practitioners when conducting an acquisition in France.

The book will give to foreign companies contemplating an acquisition in France a clear picture of the French legal and tax environment. Its reading will be of a particular interest for M & A specialists, investment bankers and lawyers specialised in cross-border acquisitions.

Charles-Henri de Pardieu
Nathalie Weyd
Paris
September 1993

List of Abbreviations

ABSA	actions avec bons de souscription d'actions
BALO	*Bulletin des Annonces Légales et Obligatoires*
CBV	Conseil des Bourses de Valeurs
COB	Commission des Opérations de Bourse
EURL	entreprise unipersonnelle à responsabilité limitée
GIE	groupement d'intérêt économique
LBO	leveraged buy-out
OBSA	obligations avec bons de souscription d'action
OP	offre publique
OPA	offre publique d'achat
OPE	offre publique d'échange
OPM	offre publique mixte
OPR	offre publique de retrait
OPV	offre publique de vente
RES	rachat d'une entreprise par ses salariés
SA	Société anonyme
SARL	Société à responsabilité limitée
SBF	Société des Bourses Françaises
SCA	Société en commandite par actions
SCS	Société en commandite simple
SICAV	Société d'investissement à capital variable
SNC	Société en nom collectif
TPI	titres au porteur identifiables

France

I. INTRODUCTION

The second half of the 1980s was a period of fast and significant development of the French business and financial scene whereas the beginning of the 1990s has been characterised by financial and economic uncertainties. During this period France has had to introduce, adapt and regulate new types of transactions and practices created in other more innovatory financial centres around the world.

The year 1984 saw the starting point of the evolutionary process, with Law No. 84–46 of 24th January 1984 which completely reorganised the banking sector. The previous law had dated back to 1945, with piecemeal amendments over the years. This was followed by a law of 11th July 1985, Article 8 of which legalised swaps and other financial instruments.

The French stock market and the financial professions were in turn reorganised by Law No. 88–70 of 22nd January 1988. Merger legislation was brought up to date by a law of 5th January 1988 amending French company law and takeover techniques were substantially modified by the law of 2nd August 1989 and implementing decrees and regulations in late 1989 and early 1990. Concentration and competition law was updated by an ordinance of 1st December 1986, which cancelled the previous ordinance of 30th June 1945. A fundamental reform of the French system of unit trusts and investment companies ("fonds communs de placement" and "sociétés d'investisement à capital variable") was introduced by the law of 2nd August 1989 and implementing regulations. Insurance legislation was modernised by Law No. 89–1014 of 31st December 1989, and exchange control regulations were gradually liberalised in 1988 and 1989 and to a very large extent lifted in early 1990.

Tax legislation was also affected by the changing environment, although evolution was less dramatic than in other sectors. Thus group tax relief was introduced by the Finance Act for 1988, and corporation tax has been consistently lowered from its 50% rate in 1986 to 33.33% for fiscal years starting in 1993, regardless of whether profits are distributed or not. More importantly the tax administration changed certain of its crippling practices and in particular abandoned the theory that a sale of 100% of the shares of a company was a sale of the company's business and should be taxed accordingly in relation to registration tax and capital gain tax. The finance laws have gradually implemented the EC tax Directives; thus the 1992 Finance Law implemented, will effect from 23rd July 1990, the EC Tax Directive 90/434 concerning the new regime for mergers, spin-offs and exchanges of shares.

Although France can now rightly claim that it has a corpus of business laws and regulations which is modern and efficient, it is nonetheless true to say that most of the changes had long been overdue.

This necessary process of adaptation started in fact slightly earlier in the late 1970s to early 1980s when French banks began to become involved in international syndicated loans and facilities and project finance. Then came the emergence of new financial instruments (swaps, options, FRAs, etc.) which was followed by the introduction and development of new equity funding techniques. This in turn fostered a sudden increase in trading on the stock exchange, coupled with a growing interest in financial markets on the part of French institutional and individual investors. This was substantially enhanced by the "privatisation" of nationalised companies in 1986 and deregulation in 1988, despite the various stock exchange crashes.

There was accordingly at this time a significant boom in merger and acquisition transactions which developed from the gradual realisation that French businesses needed to conduct a profound and long overdue restructuring of their organisations in order to occupy a competitive position in the post-1992 European market and also in the world markets.

Thus acquisitions of quoted French companies (of which there are just over 900) through the takeover bid procedure have increased from 42 over the whole period 1975–84 (i.e. an average of four each year), to 9 in 1986, 9 in 1987, 40 in 1988, 30 in 1989, 38 in 1990, 38 in 1991 and 40 in 1992. Figures for unquoted companies are difficult to obtain. However a survey has shown that acquisitions of "substantial" companies (quoted and unquoted) have increased from 284 in 1986 to 1053 in 1988. These figures suggest that acquisition activity in both quoted and non-quoted companies which had roughly quadrupled up until 1989 is currently stabilising as a result of the economic and financial recession which prevails worldwide.

Such wide-ranging changes on the business and financial scene have inevitably brought about corresponding changes in the attitudes and practices of the members of the business community and have produced a substantial quantity of amending or innovatory legislation. Business and tax lawyers have also had to adapt their structures and their drafting and negotiating techniques, as have the French courts and legal writers: these last two professions have, however, reacted more slowly and have only just started this evolutionary process. As a result progress in this field is sometimes inadequate, as subsequent developments will show.

A general overview of the corporate environment will be dealt with on p.5 *et seq*, while p.31 *et seq* will briefly address the prior administrative and other consents which must be obtained in relation to merger and acquisition transactions in France. Merger and acquisition techniques together with the taxation considerations related thereto will then be reviewed on p.39 *et seq* and 94 *et seq* respectively. Finally p.110 *et seq* will finally address issues related to labour law in the context of mergers and acquisitions.

A general overview of the corporate environment will be dealt with in sections II, followed by a brief discussion, in section III, of the prior administrative and other consents which must be obtained in relation to merger and acquisition transactions in France. Merger and acquisition techniques together with the taxation considerations related thereto will then be reviewed in sections IV and V respectively. Finally, section VI addresses issues related to labour law in the context of mergers and acquisitions.

II. CORPORATE OVERVIEW

Review of Common Forms of Business in France

The foreign investor who wishes to acquire a business or to establish a joint venture in France will find two main types of commercial company:

- the "société de capitaux" (joint stock company), where the identity of the other shareholders is not an essential factor and where the underlying principles are the limitation of liability of the shareholders to their respective contributions to the share capital and the free transfer of the shares unless specifically provided otherwise, and
- the "société de personnes" (partnership) where the identity of partners joining the company is a critical factor and where the partners' liability for the corporate debts is both joint and several and unlimited in extent.

The Commercial companies are regulated by the provisions of the Law No. 66–537 of 24th July 1966 and by the provisions of Decree No. 67–236 of 23rd March 1967 which set out a statutory framework applicable to the various types of commercial company ("French company law"). Thus shareholders have little latitude to organise their relationships within a commercial company.

It should be noted that the distinction usually made under French company law between the "sociétés de capitaux" and the "sociétés de personnes" is mitigated in practice for a number of reasons: the importance of the identity of the partners in the "sociétés de personnes" may be diminished by stipulating in the company's articles of association that, for example, the death of a partner will not result in the dissolution of the company which may survive with the partner's heirs. Conversely, in the "sociétés de capitaux", the identity of the shareholders may be reinforced by the insertion of an approval clause ("clause d'agrément") regarding transferees of the shares.

In addition to those referred to above, one should mention other forms of special entitys, such as the "groupement d'intérêt économique" (or GIE) which is a special service entity, the corporate purpose of which must be ancillary to the activities of the GIE's members. There is also the "société en participation" (silent and unincorporated partnership) which, exceptionally, is not considered as being an entity distinct from its partners.

According to tax statistics, there are approximately 700,000 commercial companies in France, varying from closely held companies to multinational conglomerates.

Medium or small-sized companies are essentially incorporated for tax and social security reasons, although the "extrepreneur" could very often, from an economic viewpoint, run his business individually without incorporating a legal entity. For this reason, the "société à responsabilité limitée" (or SARL), which offers simplicity of organisation combined with limited liability, is the most common corporate structure in France.

For large publicly held companies or for businesses requiring substantial capital investment, the "société anonyme" (or SA) is the form of incorporation traditionally used.

There are briefly set out below the main characteristics of the most common corporate forms for an investment.

"Sociétés de Personnes"

The existing commercial "sociétés de personnes" are the "société en nom collectif" (or SNC) and the société en commandite simple" (or SCS), both of which are registered with the Registry of Trade and Companies.

"Société en Nom Collectif" (SNC)
An SNC is a partnership between at least two partners who may be French or foreign individuals or legal entities. The partners are regarded as "merchants")"commerçants") and are accordingly jointly and severally liable for the corporate debts to an unlimited extent.

There is no minimum legal share capital requirement and the share capital need not be paid up immediately after the issue of the shares or by a specific deadline. The interests in the capital are represented by shares which are not freely transferable: a transfer of shares to other partners or to third parties remains subject to the unanimous consent of the other partners notwithstanding any provision to the contrary in the articles of association.

The sharing of the profits and losses is determined in the articles of association of the SNC. It is possible to allocate to one partner a proportion of the results which does not necessarily correspond to his share in the capital. The sharing of the profits may be different from the sharing of the losses. However, it is unlawful to allocate to one or several partners all the profits or all the losses, to deprive one partner of any portion of the profits or to exempt one partner from any losses.

The decision-making process is flexible, by comparison with other corporate forms: a partners' meeting must be held in the following two cases:

- for the approval of the annual accounts;
- when a meeting is convened at the request of a partner.

Unless otherwise provided by the articles of association, all other decisions may be taken by written consultation and agreement. Some decisions of the partners must be made by unanimous consent, such as the dismissal of the manager ("gérant") in certain cases, the continuation of the partnership despite the dismissal of the "gérant", the transfer of shares or the continuation of the partnership despite the bankruptcy of one of the partners. The majority rules for other decisions may be freely determined pursuant to the articles of association.

All the partners are in principle equally responsible for the company's management, including its day-to-day management. When the articles of association provide otherwise, the SNC may have one or several "gérants" (i.e. managers) who may be French or foreign individuals or legal entities, chosen among the partners whether by unanimous consent (when appointed in the articles of association) or according to the majority rules set out in the articles of association in other cases. The "gérant" is vested with all necessary power to act and to represent the company and no limitation placed on the powers of the "gérant" is binding vis-à-vis *bona fide* third parties. The "gérant" appointed by the partners may delegate part of his powers to an employee of the SNC.

The dismissal of a "gérant" chosen among the partners must be decided in principle by unanimous consent of the other partners, whereas a "gérant" who is not a partner can be dismissed by decision of a majority of the partners unless otherwise stipulated in the articles of association.

The main advantages of the SNC structure are its flexible organisation and the limited corporate formalities during the lifetime of the company. However, since the individual relationship between the partners is essential in an SNC, this type of company should only be used where the joint venture implies a close cooperation between a limited number of partners. There are also tax advantages which may determine the choice of this structure, especially as a result of the fiscal transparency of an SNC (see p.95 *et seq*).

The joint and several liability of the partners for all corporate debts and the extension of bankruptcy to all the partners if the SNC is declared bankrupt are the essential disadvantages. In addition, the transfer of SNC shares always gives rise to a registration tax of 4.80%. However, the issue of the partners' unlimited liability may be solved if the partner is a legal entity with limited liability.

"Société en Commandite Simple" (SCS)
There are two types of partner within this partnership:

- one or several general partners ("commandités") who manage the company and are jointly and severally liable for the corporate debts for an unlimited amount, as are the partners in an SNC:
- one or more limited partners ("commanditaires") who contribute to the share capital and incur a liability limited to their capital contribution provided they do not actively take part in the management of the company.

As in an SNC, there is no minimum legal share capital and the share capital does not need to be paid up. The SCS is prohibited from going public.

The shares held by the "commanditaires" in an SCS may only be transferred to another "commanditaire" or to a third party with the unanimous consent of the other "commanditaires" and of the "commandités".

However, the articles of association can validly provide that the shares of the "commanditaires" are freely transferable to other partners or can be transferred to third parties with the unaimous consent of the "commandités" and the majority of the "commanditaires".

The SCS is managed by a "géant" who may be selected from among the "commandites" or from among third parties. A "commanditaire" cannot become a "gérant" without losing his status. The rules previously set out for the appointment, dismissal and scope of authority of the "gérant" in an SNC apply equally to the "gérant" in an SCS.

The SCS is not a widely used "société de personnes" as it has the same disadvantages as the SNC, especially as regards the "commandités" (joint and several liability) without offering the same flexibility (the two-tier structure is complex with the "commandités" and "commanditaires" having different legal status) and without offering the same tax advantages, since the SCS, unlike the SNC, has no full fiscal transparency.

"Sociétés de Capitaux"

The existing types of "sociétés de capitaux" are the "société anonyme" (or SA), the "société en commandite par actions" (or SCA) and the "société à responsabilité limitée" (or SARL), this last entity being usually classified among the "sociétés de capitaux", although it has the characteristics of both the "sociétés de capitaux" and the "sociétés de personnes". The liability of the shareholders is usually limited in such companies except where they are general shareholders ("commandités") in an SCA.

The most popular forms in France are the SARL and the SA for the respective reasons set out below.

"Société Anonyme" (SA)
An SA is commercial whatever its corporate object. However, by contrast with the SNC or SCS, its shareholders do not acquire the status of merchant. The shareholders' liability is limited to their respective contributions to the share capital.

An SA requires a minimum of seven shareholders, but there is no maximum. The shareholders may be French or foreign individuals or legal entities.

The minimum share capital for a privately held SA is FF 250,000 divided into shares whereas the minimum requirement is FF 1,500,000 for a company going public. The minimum par value per share may be freely determined by the articles of association.

The contributions to the share capital made by shareholders may be contributions in cash and/or in kind.

Shares representing a contribution-in-kind must be totally paid up at the time they are issued. Shares representing a contribution in cash may be partly paid up (subject to a minimum of 25% of the par value of each share) at the time they are issued, the remaining amount being paid up over the next five years as and when called by the board of directors. Any subscription premium should be entirely paid up upon subscription. An SA may issue negotiable bonds.

The management of an SA can be structured in two different ways: an SA may either have a board of directors ("conseil d'administration") with a president of the board of directors (the traditional form) or it may have a two-tier management structure (double-tier form) with a directorate ("directoire") working under the control of a supervisory board ("conseil de surveillance:).

The board of directors is composed of a minimum of 3 and a maximum of 12 members (15 if the company is quoted) chosen from among the shareholders. Directors may be either French or foreign individuals or legal entities. When a company is a director, it must appoint a permanent representative who incurs the same liability as if he were a director.

The board of directors must appoint among its members, by passing a resolution of a majority of the members present or represented, a president who must be an individual and who can be assisted by one or two general managers. The company can have two general managers if the share capital exceeds FF 500,000.

The president of the board of directors and the general manager(s) may always be removed at will by a majority of the board of directors and are not entitled to any form of compensation when dismissed from their functions, unless the dismissal is particularly injurious or unless they have an employment contract.

The board of directors is vested with the broadest powers to act in the name of the SA. However the board of directors in practice merely oversees the president and the general manager(s) who manage the company and who have full power vis-à-vis third parties without notice.

In the double-tier form of the SA, the company is managed by the directorate under the continuous supervision of the members of the supervisory board composed of 3–12 members chosen among the shareholders.

The directorate has a minimum of two members and a maximum of five (seven in quoted companies) appointed by the supervisory board by a majority of the members present or represented. If the company's share capital is lower than FF 1,000,000, the directorate may consist of a single member.

The directorate is composed only of individuals. Furthermore, members of the directorate cannot be members of the supervisory board.

Members of the directorate receive better protection than members of the board of directors because, by contrast with members of the board of directors, they can be removed from office only by vote of a general shareholders' meeting, upon the proposal of the supervisory board. A dismissal without proper cause ("juste motif") may give rise to damages. Even if the shareholders' control over the members of the directorate is really effective, the fact that the supervisory board cannot remove members of the directorate which it itself nominates represents a fetter on its supervisory power.

The directorate is vested with power to perform any act in the name of the company and any limitations set out in the articles of association are unforceable against third parties without notice.

As French company law does not provide for the internal organisation of the directorate, the articles of association may freely determine (unlike in the traditional form of SA) when the directorate must meet, the conditions on which a proxy may be given or the quorum and majority required to pass resolutions. Furthermore, it should be noted that there are no legal requirements as to the number of meetings.

This double-tier form of SA separates management from ownership in a way which enables independent professionals to manage the company. These professional managers can enter into employment contracts with the company and thereby obtain greater job security. If removed by the shareholders without appropriate justification, these managers can obtain damages.

The supreme authority in an SA lies with the shareholders' meeting. The shareholders must be consulted on any decision which exceeds the scope of authority of the directors.

Any shareholder is entitled to attend general meetings if he has paid up his shares to the extent required by the board of directors. However, the articles of association may require that a shareholder own a minimum number of shares — no more than 10 — in order to attend ordinary general shareholders' meetings.

Each shareholder has the same number of voting rights as the shares he owns or represents although shares without voting rights may exist as described below and although some companies' articles of association may restrict the voting rights allocated to each shareholder (see p.88 below).

Any resolution which does not require an extraordinary shareholders' meeting under the articles of association or under French company law may be passed by the ordinary shareholders' meeting.

Resolutions are passed by a majority of one half of the votes present or represented. French company law and French case law do not accept videoed conference meetings or meetings on "paper" (i.e. where there is no physical attendance of the members) and a shareholder may require the cancellation of any resolutions passed at such a meeting (as a result of failure to obtain the necessary quorum and the majority required to validly pass the resolutions).

The ability of a shareholder to command 50% of the voting rights accordingly confers upon such shareholder control of the appointment of the management and of approval of the annual accounts, both of which are passed by a majority vote of the shareholders. However, absolute control of an SA entails the ability to pass extraordinary resolutions by a majority of two-thirds of the voting rights present or represented. Extraordinary resolutions are required to amend the articles of association.

Certain decisions cannot be made by a simple decision of the extraordinary meeting because unanimous consent of all shareholders is required (such as the decision to transform the company into a "société en nom collectif" or the decision to increase the share capital through an increase in the par value of the shares).

The shares of an unquoted SA must be registered shares ("action nominatives") whereas shares of a quoted SA may be in bearer form ("actions au porteur") or in registered form.

Registered shares can either be placed into accounts maintained by the issuing company ("nominatifs purs") or they are put into accounts held by an agent (a bank or duly qualified broker) appointed by the issuer of the shares ("nominatifs administrés"). Shares of quoted companies can also be in an identifiable bearer form ("titres au porteur identifiables" or TPI) which enables the issuing company to know the holder of each share, it being understood that the issue of such securities must be expressly provided for in the company's articles of association and that such shares can only be securities with voting rights at shareholders' meetings, i.e. ordinary shares, "obligations avec bons de souscriptions d'actions" (or OBSA), "actions avec bons de souscriptions d'actions" (or ABSA).

An SA may have several different classes of shares. In addition to ordinary shares, an SA may create preferred shares. A preferred share generally gives financial advantages over an ordinary share, such as:

- a larger share in the profits;
- a preferred dividend;
- a larger part in any liquidation premium.

Preferred shares may also be deprived of voting rights only if the issuing company has realised distributable profits during the two financial years preceding the creation of such shares. Preferred shares without voting rights cannot represent more than one quarter of the share capital and cannot be owned by the directors of the company. These preferred shares without any voting rights give a right to a preferred dividend, the minimum of which is fixed by the law.

An SA may also issue shares with double voting rights in favour of all the registered shares which are fully paid up and recorded under the name of the same shareholder for a minimum of two successive years. A shareholder may however waive the benefit of this right. Some companies also grant an increased dividend (by approximately 10%) to any shareholder who has kept his registered shares fully paid up or for a minimum two-year period. However, a bill is expected to be submitted to the Senate in the coming months which would regulate the conditions of payment of an increased dividend to shareholders.

In addition to the right to vote, each ordinary share gives a right to the corporate assets and profits to an extent equal to the number of shares held, unless otherwise provided by the articles of association. It is nevertheless unlawful to allocate to one or several shareholders all the profits of the company or to deprive a shareholder of any share in the profits.

Sharing in the losses does not need to be proportional to the shares held provided a shareholder's liability cannot exceed his contribution to the share capital and provided a shareholder cannot be exempt from any sharing in a company's losses.

Unlike a "société de personnes", the underlying principle in an SA is the free transfer of the shares. However, the articles of association may provide for some limitation on the transfer of shares, bearing in mind that no shareholder should be prevented from withdrawing from the company if and when he decides to do so. The following limitations are often included in the company's articles of association:

- prior approval by the board of directors of the company before any share transfer takes place ("clause d'agrément"), though this provision cannot apply to transfers of shares between shareholders, spouses, predecessors and descendants;
- preemptive rights ("droits de préemption");
- a prohibition against selling any shares during a certain period of time justified by the company's interests ("clause d'interdiction temporaire de cession");
- an obligation on a shareholder to sell all his shares in case of specific events defined in the articles of association ("clause de rachat forcé").

However, the "Commission des Opérations de Bourse" (COB) (see p.73 *et seq*) requires that such clauses be deleted from the company's articles of association if the company is quoted on the Stock Exchange.

An SA must appoint at least one statutory auditor and a substitute statutory auditor. Two statutory auditors are required in any SA whose accounts are consolidated.

Although the administration of an SA is cumbersome and inflexible (in particular for shareholders' meetings), the SA is an appropriate form for a business whose capital requirements cannot be met by a limited number of shareholders or which needs to offer negotiable shares or bonds to finance its development. This is the reason why the SA is such a popular corporate form in France (there being approximately 100,000 of them) covering essentially middle-sized or large public companies.

The traditional form of SA with a board of directors remains the most popular form in France, although the double-tier form is most often used for SAs run by foreign companies establishing subsidiaries in France.

As the French SA does not offer much flexibility, compared with other jurisdictions, in terms of its internal corporate organisation, especially in the context of joint ventures, a simplified SA structure ("société par actions simplifiée") is to be proposed to investors in a bill currently being submitted to the Senate for enactment. According to this bill, the shareholders would have much more latitude to adapt the articles of association to their specific objectives and to establish the framework of their internal relationship. Thus, the validity of approval clauses for the transfer of shares between shareholders as well as the validity of withdrawal or exclusion clauses would be recognised. The shareholders could also freely define the composition of the management body and the conditions under which shareholders' decisions could be passed.

However, this type of simplified "société par actions" would be confirmed exclusively to privately held SAs and not to SAs intending to go public.

The simplified "société par actions" could be incorporated with only two shareholders and its minimum share capital would be FF 1,500,000, fully paid up on subscription.

"Société à Responsabilité Limitée" (SARL)

A SARL is regarded as commercial whatever its stated corporate purpose. However, its shareholders do not acquire the status of merchant. The shareholders' liability is limited to their respective contributions to the share capital.

A SARL requires only one shareholder (in such a case the SARL is called an "enterprise unipersonnelle à responsabilité limitée: or EURL) but cannot have more than 50 shareholders. The shareholders may be French or foreign individuals or legal entities.

The minimum share capital is FF 50,000 divided into shares with a par value of at least FF 100, each of which must be totally paid up at the time they are issued. The company may not issue negotiable bonds and may not go public.

A SARL is managed by one or more "gérants" who must be individuals but who need not be shareholders. The "gérants" are appointed either by the articles of association or by an ordinary shareholders' meeting when the company is incorporated by a majority of more than 50% of the shares unless the articles of association provide for a higher majority. Their term of office may be a specific duration or for an unlimited period.

A SARL "gérant" may be freely dismissed by the ordinary general shareholders' meeting by a majority of more than 50% of the shares. A dismissal may give rise to damages if not supported by good reasons.

In the absence of any provision to the contrary, the "gérant" has authority to carry out any managerial act in the company's interest. If there are several "gérants", each of them can commit the company, unless another vetoes the act.

The company is liable for the acts of the "gérant" except when these acts are outside the corporate purpose and when the company can prove that third parties knew that such acts were outside the corporate purpose. The "gérant" may delegate authority to one or several directors and appoint special or temporary representatives. A SARL "gérant" is liable for acts which violate the statutory rules and regulations governing SARLs and the company's articles of association or for serious mistakes committed while managing the company.

A general shareholders' meeting must take place in the following two cases:

- for the approval of the annual accounts;
- when a meeting is called by one or several shareholders representing either one quarter of the shareholders and one quarter of the shares or alternatively representing one half of the shares.

Unless otherwise provided in the articles of association, all other decisions may be taken by written consultation (unlike in the case of an SA).

Meetings are usually called by the "gérant" by registered letter 15 days in advance. All shareholders are entitled to attend general meetings. Each shareholder has the same number of voting rights as the number of shares he owns or represents.

Any resolution not required by the articles of association or by French company law to be passed at an extraordinary meeting may be passed by an ordinary meeting by a majority of more than 50% of the shares.

An extraordinary shareholders' meeting is required whenever the articles of association are amended. The necessary majority is more than 75% of the shares. Accordingly, absolute control of a SARL requires a holding of more than three-quarters of the shares.

Each share gives a right to its owner to the corporate assets and profits to an extent proportional to the number of shares held, unless otherwise provided by the articles of association. However, as in the case of the other corporate forms, it is unlawful to allocate all the profits to one or several shareholders or to exempt a shareholder from any losses.

The shares of a SARL are not negotiable (the transfer of shares can only be carried out by a written deed). Except as otherwise provided in the articles of association, the shares may be freely transferred between shareholders. The transfer of shares to third parties is subject to the prior approval of an extraordinary shareholders' meeting.

For middle-sized companies, the choice between limited liability companies should be essentially made between the SA and the SARL. The simplicity of the SARL over the SA is an advantage. However, by contrast with the SA, the shares are not negotiable and must be fully paid up. Furthermore the transfer of SARL shares always gives rise to registration tax at the rate of 4.80% which constitutes a deterrent from a tax viewpoint.

"Société en Commandite par Actions" (SCA)

The SCA has the same features as the SCS, except as set out below. The SCA has two different categories of partners: general partners ("commandités") and limited partners ("commanditaires") who incur different levels of liability.

However, the SCA form is also similar to that of the SA in certain respects. There is a minimum of four shareholders, including at least three "commanditaires" and one "commandité", in an SCA. Unlike the SCS, the SCA is not prohibited from going public. However, a quoted company incorporated as an SA which decides to be transformed into an SCA must withdraw from the Stock Exchange.

The minimum share capital is FF 1,500,000 for quoted SCAs

and FF 250,000 for private SCAs. The provisions concerning the share capital and the issue of shares and bonds are the same as for an SA, except that the SCA can have a variable share capital if provided for in the articles of association.

The "commanditaires" are in the same position as the shareholders of an SA with regard to their liability which is limited to the amount of their contribution and their shares which are freely negotiable and transferable under the same terms and conditions as those for the transfer of shares in an SA. Resolutions are passed by the "commanditaires" by the same majority as resolutions passed by the shareholders of an SA.

The "commandités" are in the same legal position as the partners of an SNC. If not appointed as "gérants" of the SCA, they may nevertheless have access twice a year to the company's accounts and submit questions in writing regarding the management. Furthermore, they are entitled to receive a portion of the benefits which may be freely determined in the articles of association.

The management of the SCA is carried out by a "gérant" appointed from among the "commandités" from or among third parties with the unanimous consent of the "commandités" and a 50% majority of the "commanditaires", unless otherwise provided in the articles of association. The conditions of dismissal of the "gérant" may be freely determined in the articles of association. The articles of association often provide that the decision of the "commandités" to dismiss the "gérant" should be taken with unanimous consent.

The SCA has a supervisory board composed of at least three members who may not be "commandités".

The supervisory board's mission is to assume the permanent supervision of the management of the company. It does not play a management role but merely controls the corporate decisions together with the company's statutory auditors and submits an annual report with its recommendations to the annual general meeting of shareholders.

The members of the supervisory board are appointed either by the founders, in the case of a quoted company, or by the first ordinary shareholders' meeting and during the life of the company, by the ordinary general shareholders' meeting. As opposed to the shareholders' meeting appointing the "gérant", the "commandités" are not allowed to participate in the vote appointing the members of the supervisory board.

The term of office of the members is fixed by the articles of association. Unless the articles of association provide otherwise, the members of the supervisory board may be dismissed at any time by the ordinary general meeting of shareholders without cause (as is the case for directors of an SA). Conversely, the members of the supervisory board may resign without justification.

The SCA form has become more popular in the last decade as it enables a separation between capital and the management, which remains independent, and as it offers flexibility in terms of corporate organisation. An established management trying to secure sources of funding while maintaining its independence (such as in the leveraged buy-out technique) may thus have an interest in opting for the SCA form. This structure where the "commandités" and the "gérants" are quasi-irrevocable is also appropriate if the company wishes to protect itself from hostile takeover bids. However, the decision to transform an existing SA into an SCA should be carefully considered, especially if the SA is already quoted, as this results in the delisting of the company.

Other Types of Corporate Structures

"Groupement d'Intérêt Economique" (GIE)

The GIE is governed by Ordinance No. 67.821 of 23rd September 1967 which aims to enable companies to pool their resources while remaining independent. It is a legal entity with at least two members, which is distinct from its members, although it is not a company. The members may be French or foreign individuals or legal entities.

A GIE must carry out an economic activity which may be either civil or commercial. The GIE activity must be an extension of and ancillary to the activity of its members, which restricts significantly the use of this structure for joint ventures.

A GIE is not intended to make profits per se, although it may make such profits in the normal course of its business. There is no capital requirement. However, a GIE may receive contributions in cash or in kind from its members. A GIE may issue bonds if all its members are companies authorised to issue bonds.

It can be managed either by individuals or by legal entities which must appoint an individual as permanent representative. The members can freely determine in the articles of association the number of directors, the way they will be appointed, their terms of office and the conditions for their appointment and removal. The directors are jointly and severally liable if they commit any fault in the management or if they do not comply with the articles of association or the legal provisions which regulate GIE.

The members have the greatest flexibility to organise within the articles of association the rules relating to general members' meetings (scope of authority, majority, quorum, etc.) as well as the rules regarding the appointment and power of the GIE's controller. Unless otherwise provided in the articles of association, the unanimous consent of the members is required for the acceptance of new members.

The GIE is a flexible structure and there are no cumbersome formalities with respect to its creation or operation. The fiscal transparency of the GIE is an additional tax advantage. One of the most notable companies which has chosen this form is Airbus Industries. However, the GIE is not as commonly used as it could be in the context of joint ventures for a number of reasons:

- its members are jointly and severally liable for the debts which the GIE may incur in the completion of its corporate purpose (the GIE may nevertheless ask the contractor to waive the members' liability and agree only to pursue the group itself);
- should the GIE be declared bankrupt, the bankruptcy would then be extended to all its members
- the activity of the GIE must be ancillary to the activity of its members and can neither be substituted for this activity nor be a new one.

"Société en Participation

A "société en participation" is similar to a silent partnership. It is not a legal entity and is therefore not subject to any registration formalities. It can be deemed to be either of a commercial or civil nature, depending on its activity. Its existence should, in principle, remain unknown to third parties.

In such a case, only the active partner commits himself vis-à-vis these third parties. However, in the case of deficiency, the "silent partner" would be called upon by the active partner to contribute his share of the losses incurred. It is generally felt that third parties can take no action against silent partners if the existence of the "société en participation" is not disclosed. The main advantages of this kind of arrangement are its flexibility and its confidentiality.

Rights of the Minority Shareholders

Where an investor acquires less than 100% of the share capital of a company, his rights to exercise an influence on the decision-making process in the company depend on his level of participation as well as on the legal form of such a company.

Minority Shareholders' Protection in the "Sociétés de Capitaux"

Minority Shareholder: Over 33.33% or 25%

A minority shareholder, provided he holds just over 33.33% of the voting rights of an SA or an SCA or 25% of the voting rights of a SARL, may veto decisions and actions which require for their validity the prior authorisation of an extraordinary general meeting of shareholders. Such decisions include the following:

- all amendments to the articles of association of the company (in particular any increase or reduction of the share capital, any transfer of the registered office, any change in the company's purpose, any change in the number of directors, any inclusion of or amendment to clauses restricting transfers of shares);
- acts of disposal or transfer of the business of the company or of its major assets or a substantial part of the company's assets (see p. 68–69 *et seq.*);
- merger transactions and partial transfers of business in consideration for shares of another company;
- issue of convertible bonds.

Repeated or unjustified exercise by the minority shareholders of his right of veto (assuming it is available) may entail the invalidity of the vote of such shareholder if it can be proved to a court that the shareholder was acting in his own personal interest and against the interests of the company. The minority shareholder may also be held liable in damages to the other shareholders. However, only very serious circumstances could persuade a court to hold a minority shareholder liable.

A shareholder of an SA who holds over 25% of the share

capital of the company, can oppose the transformation of an SA into a SARL.

Minority Shareholder: At Least 10%

A minority shareholder who holds at least 10% of the share capital of an SA, SCA or SARL can exercise the following rights:

- cause the appointment of a judicial agent ("mandataire judiciaire") to convene a general shareholders' meeting (irrespective of the size of his shareholding in the case of shareholders of a SARL) provided the request complies with the company's interests;
- submit twice a year written questions to the board or to the "gérant" on facts which may jeopardise the company's business (irrespective of the size of his shareholding in the case of shareholders of a SARL);
- require dismissal or judicial revocation of the company's auditor;
- cause a judicial investigator ("expert judiciaire") to be appointed by the court in order to review and appraise certain actions or decisions of the management of the company. This is in general a way of obtaining clear evidence of mismanagement with a view to an action in damages against the director of the "gérant".

Minority Shareholder: At least 5%

A minority shareholder holding at least 5% (with other minority shareholders) of the share capital of an SA or SCA has the following rights:

- to ask for written questions to be addressed to the shareholders' meeting; where the share capital exceeds FF 5m, the minimum percentage is reduced from 4% to 0.50%;
- to exercise on his own behalf and on behalf of other minority shareholders (if they together own not less than 5% of the share capital) the so-called "action sociale". Where the share capital of an SA or SCA exceeds FF 5m, the

minimum percentage is reduced from 4% down o.50%.

Minority Shareholder and the "Action Sociale"

A minority shareholder of a SARL may start the "action sociale" on his own behalf and on behalf of other minority shareholders if they together own at least 10% of the share capital. It should be noted that the "action sociale" may also be started individually by any minority shareholder of an SA, SCA or SARL irrespective of the shareholding.

The "action sociale" is an action of the company against the management which is exercised on behalf of the company by a shareholder or a group of shareholders. The action will result in damages being awarded to the company (and not to the shareholder) if successful. It is necessary to prove the loss incurred by the company and the fault or negligence of the management.

The "action sociale" should be distinguished from the "action individuelle" which may be started by any shareholder or third party against the management and which aims at compensating the plaintiff for the individual loss he allegedly incurred.

Minority Shareholder: Single Share

Ultimately a minority shareholder holding a single share in the share capital of an SA, SCA or SARL has the right to ask written questions to the board or to the "gérant" during the period preceding the shareholders' meeting. He may also cause the appointment of a judicial agent to convene a general shareholders' meeting (in case of urgency only) or obtain from the court an order cancelling a decision made by the majority shareholder at a shareholders' meeting which required unanimous consent or which was in the exclusive interests of the majority shareholder but contrary to the interests of the company and to the detriment of the minority shareholders.

A shareholder may also, regardless of the size of his shareholding, require the court to appoint a judicial agent who will manage the company in lieu of the existing management. However, such an action will be successful only in cases where specific circumstances evidence the fact that the day-to-day management of the company has been rendered impossible, for example by reason of a deadlock at the board of directors or a misuse by the majority shareholders of their rights such as to endanger the company's interests.

In practice the courts are rather reluctant to appoint a judicial administrator when the company's interests are not endangered over a short time period. However, French courts may, when the company's interests seem to be at risk and when there appears to be a fundamental disagreement between the shareholders, decide to prohibit the company's directors over a specific period from doing any managerial act which may have irrevocable consequences for the company and at the same time to appoint a judicial agent ("mandataire de justice") to attend shareholders' meetings or the board of directors' meetings with a view to supervising any failure to comply with such prohibition.

Minority Shareholders' Protection in Quoted Companies

In addition to the rights referred to above, special protection is granted to minority shareholders of a company whose shares are quoted on the official market or on the second market. A minority shareholder, regardless of the size of his shareholding in the quoted company, may require the Conseil des Bourses de Valeurs (CBV) to cause the majority shareholders to submit a public offer to purchase the shares held by the minority shareholders under an "offre de retrait" (see p. 84 *et seq.* below). This procedure enables the minority shareholders to withdraw from a quoted company, especially when the market is no longer liquid as a result of the prevailing position of one or seveal shareholders holding at least 95% of the voting rights in the general meeting.

Furthermore, protection of minority shareholders in companies with shares quoted on the official or on the second market is ensured through the increased financial information required by the Commission des Opérations de Bourse (or COB)(see p.73 *et seq.*below) to be made available to the public (including the minority shareholders):

- the company's annual accounts, the proposed distribution of profits and the consolidated accounts, if available, must be published in the *Bulletin des Annonces Légales et Obligatoires* or (BALO), a special legal gazette, within the four months following the close of the financial year and at least 15 days before the annual ordinary general meeting of shareholders; a second publication must be made within the 45 days following the annual shareholders' meeting, when the annual accounts certified by the statutory auditors have been approved by the shareholders and the profits have been distributed;
- the company's half-year results (on a consolidated basis for companies with consolidated accounts) accompanied by a certificate from the statutory auditors on the fairness of the information provided must be published in the BALO within the four months following the end of the accounting period.

The turnover for the past quarter (on a consolidated basis if the company has consolidated accounts) must be published in the BALO within the 45 days following the end of each quarter. Furthermore, such companies must also publish information concerning any increase in their share capital or any significant corporate decision. The 50% subsidiaries of companies whose shares are quoted on the official market must also (provided they meet certain conditions) publish their annual accounts and their proposed distribution of profits in a legal gazette and in the BALO.

Failure on the part of quoted companies or their subsidiaries to comply with the information referred to above is punishable by a fine of FF 3000 to FF 6000 payable by the president, directors, general managers or "gérants" of the relevant companies. It should be noted that non-French companies, even when quoted in France, are not subject to the above obligations. However, they must ensure that the French market receives information similar to the information given on the other foreign markets and they must provide the French market with certain minimal information (such as significant changes in the company, company's annual accounts.

Pursuant to COB Regulation 90–02, any company whose shares are quoted on the official market or on the second market must advise the public as early as possible of any significant fact which may have an impact on the value of its quoted shares except when the publication of such information might have a negative effect on the company's legitimate interests; in such a case the company may decide to postpone publication for confidentiality purposes provided the company is able to keep such information confidential.

Any person preparing to implement a financial transaction likely to have a significant impact on the value of the quoted shares must as early as possible inform the public of the nature of such transaction unless publication thereof is postponed for confidentiality reasons by the relevant persons.

Minority Shareholders' Protection in the "Sociétés de Personnes"

As most resolutions are passed in principle with the uninimous consent of the shareholders in this type of company, the minority shareholders cannot exercise the same degree of influence as in a "société de capitaux". However, the extent of their influence essentially depends on the provisions of the articles of association, which can freely determine the majority required for passing specific resolutions (except for those resolutions requiring the unanimous consent of the shareholders by virtue of the law referred to above).

A minority shareholder, regardless of the size of his shareholding has the following rights:

- he may require the judicial dismissal of the "gérant" provided he can prove there are legitimate grounds for such dismissal;
- he may also require the president of the commercial court to order the judicial liquidation of the company or to exercise an "action sociale" against the management.

III. REGULATORY AND OTHER AUTHORISATIONS

Investment Authorisation

Despite a number of recent liberalisation measures, foreign investment controls have not been completely lifted in France. In particular certain types of investment and investors from certain countries still need to obtain prior authorisation and in a number of other cases a prior declaration must be filed.

Pursuant to a decree of 15th January 1990 related to foreign investments control, any foreign direct investment in France made by non-EC investors is in principle subject to the prior authorisation of the Treasury Department ("Direction du Trésor) at the Ministry of Economy and Finance. The authorisation is regarded as given if the Treasury Department has not replied within one month from the date the application submitted to it. The Treasury may also choose to reply before the expiry of this one-month period either to refuse or to authorise the investment.

A direct investment is defined as:

(a) the acquisition, creation or extension of a "fonds de commerce", a branch or an individual firm;
(b) any other transaction which results in a person (or persons) acquiring control over a company having industrial, agricultural, commercial, financial or real estate activities, or extending such activities or control. Control is defined as a 20% participation in a quoted French company or a 33.33% participation in a non-quoted company.

A decree dated 11th February 1992 has facilitated the processing of investment authorisations especially for small and medium-sized investments; a direct investment of the type referred to above carried out by a non-EC investor is free and is consequently exempt from prior authorisation when its amount is less than FF 50m and when it is carried out in respect of an existing company whose turnover (together with the turnover of companies under its control) does not exceed FF 500m. However, the non-EC investor is required to file a prior declaration with the Treasury Department which will check, within 15 days following receipt of the declaration, whether the transaction is eligible for this exemption. If the Treasury Department notifies the non-EC investor that the proposed investment is not eligible for the free regime, the declaration is treated as an application for authorisation subject to the one-month procedure.

No prior authorisation (or declaration) is required for the following operations:

- creation of a branch office or a new company;
- increase by a foreign shareholder of its participation in a French company where such investor already holds 66.66% or more of the shares;

- subscription for new shares issued as a result of a capital increase provided the overall percentage holding of the investor is not increased;
- mergers, contributions of assets, sale of a business or management leases between French companies belonging to the same group (i.e. where companies are 50% subsidiaries of the same parent);
- loans, facilities, guarantees, consolidations or debt write-offs in favour of a French company by the foreign controlling shareholder;
- acquisition of interests in French real estate companies other than construction companies;
- (within a FF 10m limit) investments in small firms carrying out craft, hotel, retailing or small trade businesses;
- acquisition of agricultural land, with the exception of wine-growing concerns.

Investments by EC investors require only the filing of a prior declaration with the Treasury Department which will then check that the investor qualifies as an EC investor. If no reply has been received within 15 days the investor is regarded as approved. If the investor does not qualify as an EC investor this is notified to him and the declaration is treated as an application for authorisation subject to the one-month procedure described for non-EC investors.

Qualification as an EC investor is conditional upon the company being effectively established in the EC or controlled ultimately by persons or companies established in the EC. In this respect control is defined as ownership of 50% or more of the shares of the investor company. However if a shareholder holding less than 50% of the capital has the right to appoint the board of directors, or is able to influence the voting, or has an option over balance of the share capital, or is able to exert an influence on the decision-making process through financial arrangements, he is regarded as having control.

EC investors recognised as such and whose turnover during their last fiscal year has been in excess of FF 1bn may apply for a permanent recognition of EC investor status provided they have carried on a *bona fide* economic activity over at least three fiscal years. Such recognition removes the need for a prior declaration when subsequent investments are made. In all cases, a report must be sent to the Treasury Department at the Ministry of Economy and Finance within 20 days following completion of the transaction, with the exception of the creation of a company whose initial share capital is less than FF 5m. Investments in fields which have a connection with the exercise of public authority, public order, public health, public security or military equipment are not subject to the prior declaration procedure and require a prior authorisation subject to the one-month procedure described for non-EC firms.

Foreign Business Card ("Carte de Commerçant Étranger")

A non-French individual (unless he is an EC national or holds a residence permit) must hold a foreign business card when exercising the following functions in a French company

- partner liable for the corporate debts to an unlimited extent in an SNC, SCS OR SCA
- "gérant" in a SARL
- president of the board of directors or general manager of an SA
- president of directorate ("directoire") or general manager of an SA with the structure of directorate and supervisory board;
- director of a GIE.

This card must be obtained from the local French authorities ("préfecture") where the company carries out its activities and takes a minimum six-month period to obtain.

Competition Council Clearance

The French Competition Act (Ordinance of 1st December 1986) also regulates business "concentrations". A concentration is defined as a transaction, whatever its form or structure, which results in the transfer of the ownership or right of enjoyment of all or part of the assets of a business, or which is aimed at enabling a firm or a group of firms to exercise a significant influence, directly or indirectly, on one or several other firms.

Any concentration, or proposed concentration, within the above definition which may affect competition, in particular by the creation or reinforcement of a dominant position, may be submitted by the Minister of Economy and Finance to the Competition Council. However this prior clearance requirement only applies where the firms involved in the concentration have a share of at least 25% of the national market for relevant goods or services or of a substantial part of such a market, or alternatively have achieved a turnover (excluding taxes) exceeding FF 7bn provided in this case that at least two of the firms concerned have achieved a turnover of at least FF 2bn.

The parties to the concentration may opt for a prior submission of the proposed transaction to the Ministry of Economy and Finance. They may also notify the transaction voluntarily within three months of the effective date of the transaction. If the Minister has not replied within two months of the notification the transaction is regarded as having been approved. If the Minister decides to refer the transaction to the Competition Council, the latter then has a six-month period to review the transaction and to issue its recommendations to the Minister. Failure to reply within the stated period is also regarded as implicit authorisation.

When reviewing the operation the Competition Council has to determine whether the distortions to competition can be compensated by potential beneficial effects on economic progress. The Council also has to take into consideration the competitiveness of the companies concerned in relation to international competition.

Upon receipt of the recommendation of the Competition Council the Minister of Economy may either prohibit the concentration or authorise it subject to certain alterations designed to preserve competition or to enhance economic progress. If the Competition Council finds that there has been an abuse of dominant position, it may request the Ministry of Economy and Finance to amend, supplement or terminate within a specified period the agreements implementing the concentration through which such abuses have been made possible. This right of intervention of the Competition Council exists even where the concentration has been referred to the Ministry of Economy and Finance by the parties.

In the absence of voluntary referral, the Ministry of Economy and Finance may decide at any time without limitation to refer the matter spontaneously to the Competition Council. Failure by the parties to defer to the instructions of the Ministry of Economy and Finance exposes them to a fine equal to a maximum of 5% of the turnover in France for the latest fiscal year.

"Comité d'Entreprise" Consultation

In firms employing 50 employees or more, there must be formed a "comité d'entreprise" (workers' council) comprising elected representatives of the employees, the number of whom varies according to the size of the staff. A separate committee must be set up in each branch or plant ("comité d'etablissement") as well as a "comité de groupe" in certain groups of companies. The "comité d'entreprise" meets regularly and has the right to be informed (and sometimes consulted) on the economic activities and situation of the company, on working conditions and safety and generally on all questions relating to employment.

With specific regard to acquisitions, Article L.432–1 of the Labour Code provides that the "comité d'entreprise" must be consulted on any changes in the economic or legal organisation of the firm, and in particular in connection with a proposed merger, sale of the business or significant modification of the production structure, as well as on proposed sales or acquisitions of subsidiaries. The "comité d'entreprise" must also be consulted when the company acquires a participation (defined as a 10% interest or more) in another company and must be informed of participations acquired in the company. Takeover bids must be notified immediately to the "comité d'entreprise", which then has a right to require the offeror to appear at one of its meetings to supply additional details and to answer questions.

Transactions involving the sale of all or almost all the shares of the company and a change of management are regarded by the courts as a sale of the business and require prior consultation of the committee.

Consultation merely entitles the committee to issue a positive or negative recommendation, but not to veto or stay the proposed transaction. However in certain cases the committee may apply to the court for the appointment of an expert to review and report on one or more actions or decisions of the management. A proposed merger or acquisition could in these circumstances be considerably delayed.

Failure to consult or properly to inform the "comité d'entreprise" is a criminal offence ("délit d'entrave") punishable by a fine of up to FF 20,000 and/or up to one year's imprisonment, but this will not invalidate the transaction.

Regulated Activities

In addition to the above rules which are applicable to all acquisitions, a specific authorisation must be applied for where the target company is active in certain sectors protected by special legislation and supervised by the government. Such activities include banking, insurance, mining, newspapers, transport, telecommunications and military equipment. Generally the Treasury Department of the Ministry of Economy and Finance will refer the matter to the relevant ministry where an investment application has been filed. It is, however, preferable for the proposed acquirer to submit the relevant application personally.

A summary of authorisation for EC and non-EC investors is given below.

Investment Authorisation:

1. EC Investors

With the status of permanent EC investor

- investment is free
- exempt from prior disclosure
- simple report is required after completion of the investment.

Others

- investment is free
- prior disclosure
- 15-day period for the Treasury Department to verify whether the investment is an EC investment.

Non-EC Investors

Investments for an amount lower than FF 50m in companies with a maximum turnover of FF 500m

- investment is free;
- exempt from prior disclosure
- 15-day period for the Treasury Department to review whether the investment is in compliance with the above conditions.

Other investments

- prior disclosure (save for specific transactions which are exempt under the circular of 15th January 1990)
- implicit approval of the investment within a one-month period except in the case of a postponement by the Treasury Department.

IV. MERGER AND ACQUISITION TECHNIQUES

General Overview

Asset and Share Acquisitions

In France as elsewhere control of a company's assets can be secured by means of either a direct purchase of the assets or an acquisition of the shares of the company owning these assets. Two options are available within each alternative: assets can be purchased for cash ("cession de fonds de commerce" — see p.43 *et seq.*) or exchanged for shares ("fusion", "scission" and "apport partiel d'actif" — see p.50 *et seq.*. Share transactions can also give rise to a cash or share consideration, but the essential distinction here is between transactions in shares of companies quoted on the stock exchange (see p.57 *et seq.*) and those relating to shares of unquoted companies (see p.61 *et seq.*). Variations on the above techniques which do not significantly alter applicable rules have not been dealt with in the following developments (e.g. where a company contributes part of its assets to another in return for shares but does not use the "apport partiel d'actif" procedure set out at p.56 *et seq.*).

Joint Venture Agreements

Similarly joint ventures will not be examined in detail in the following pages because although they are a means of securing a certain degree of control over a company they do not fall strictly within the definition of mergers and acquisitions. Joint ventures in France are usually implemented by the creation of a joint company owned by the parties to the joint venture. Where ownership is 50/50 neither party has control of the decision-making process from a legal point of view. Accordingly there is in general a shareholders' agreement which sets out the agreed management policy over a number of years and contains the undertaking of the parties not to vote against certain listed decisions. Conversely where one party owns 51% or more of the shares, that party is technically in control of the decision-making process for the ordinary resolutions passed by shareholders (whereas extraordinary resolutions are passed by a qualified majority of two-thirds of the voting rights in an SA or a SCA and three-quarters of the shares in a SARL as set out on p.10 *et seq.* above), and the shareholders' agreement usually contains the commitment that certain listed decisions are not to be made without the prior consent of the minority shareholder. It should be noted that although the law does not explicitly prohibit such agreements, according to current case law, agreements whereby a shareholder, or a member of the board of directors or directorate is committed in advance to vote in a specific manner are unenforceable against third parties — including the company itself when the shareholder is totally deprived of his voting rights. The underlying principle here is the free exercise by each shareholder of his voting rights.

However, a voting agreement concluded for a limited period of time which is not against the company's interests and the sole purpose of which is not the payment of compensation is enforceable against the parties to the agreement. The party in breach may then be exposed to damages for an amount determined by the courts.

"Portage"

An alternative method of structuring such joint ventures involves the use of a "portage" contract: this is an arrangement whereby a third party (usually a bank) holds a small percentage of the shares, such percentage however being sufficient to give control to one of the other parties when added to that other party's shareholding. The third party shareholder is usually granted a put option, on a confidential basis, by the shareholder with whom the arrangement has been made and undertakes contractually to that shareholder to use his votes at shareholders' meetings in the manner indicated by the shareholder. The price of the put option is normally equal to the value of the shares plus a negotiated commission representing the remuneration of the service thus rendered. The difficulty with such an arrangement is that the validity of the put option can sometimes be challenged if the purchaser alone is committed to acquire at a fixed price. There is a further difficulty that the voting commitment may be unenforceable. The rationale here is that when the beneficiary of the put option can sell his shares at a fixed price, this is a means of protecting the beneficiary against the effects of corporate losses.

Such clauses ("clauses léonines") allegedly violate the provisions of Article 1844–1 of the Civil Code. In spite of this there is currently a tendancy to recognise the validity of the "portage" as such, although there is as yet no established case law on the subject. In any event, the introduction of the trust concept into French law which is scheduled for the near future (a bill if currently being proposed to the French Parliament) will probably decrease the significance of the "portage". It is too early at this stage to provide an introduction to this future law. However the trust concept based on a separation of ownership, which was hitherto unknown under French law, will probably give rise to new opportunities in the French business environment even though the current bill does not provide for specific tax advantages.

Finally two other issues — relating to the financing of mergers and acquisitions and legal and financial audits — will be discussed in detail in the following section. These do not raise any particular difficulties under French law. The financing and audit techniques used in France are by and large the same as those used in other jurisdictions. As regards finance, certain precautions must be taken when using the leveraged buy-out technique and these are discussed in paras below. Legal and financial audits are often carried out in the case of substantial acquisitions but infrequently in the case of small or medium-size transactions.

Asset Acquisitions

Two types of transfers are available: the transfer of assets for cash and the transfer of assets for shares. The first category is classified as a sale ("cession de fonds de commerce") and, in addition to specific laws governing this type of transaction, the French general law of sales (Articles 1582 to 1657 of the Civil Code) are also applicable. The second category covers merger transactions ("fusions et scissions") and generally involves the transfer of all of a company's assets to one or to several others, with the attendant consequence of the disappearance of the "selling" company. Mergers are regulated by a specific section of French company law.

Apart from commercial or strategic considerations, the choice between these two types of transfer is largely governed by the tax and legal implications of each. This aspect will be dealt with in greater detail below. Suffice it to say here that the sale of a "fonds de commerce" entails a registration tax at the rate of 14.2% on the value of the assets (both tangible and intangible) transferred, as well as immediate taxation of capital gains, while mergers, in most cases, do not give rise to such liabilities. In spite of this substantial drawback, a sale of the "fonds de commerce" is usually used where a seller either runs his business individually, without incorporating a company, or prefers to receive cash, and/or does not wish to remain involved in any way, whether as a shareholder or as a guarantor, with the business he has transferred. In fact, the purchaser of a "fonds de commerce" in principle acquires only assets and the seller is thus not requested to deliver warranty and indemnity provisions in favour of the purchaser as in the case of share acquisitions (see p.62 *et seq.* below).

Sale of Assets

The "Fonds de Commerce"

Although it is often loosely equated with a "business" a "fonds de commerce" is strictly a collection of assets, tangible and intangible, which enables a person or company to operate a business of a commercial or industrial nature. It has a legal existence which is distinct from that of its constituent parts, and is classified as moveable property which may, as such, be sold, leased or charged in its own right.

There is no definition of the "fonds de commerce" in the law. In practice the courts have narrowed down its composition to the existence of a "clientèle" (clients) which is the core asset of the "fonds de commerce". In addition to this intangible asset, the parties can agree to include other assets related to the "clientèle", e.g. certain tangible assets (machines, furniture and equipment, fixtures and fittings, inventories) and certain intangible assets (trade names, leases and intellectual property rights). It will at once be obvious that the "fonds de commerce", as French law understands it, does not include *per se* title to real property ("immeubles"), receivables or contractual rights. These must accordingly be specifically mentioned in the contract of sale if they are to be included in the transfer as well as the inventories which are subject to a specific tax regime (see p.109 *et seq.*). Real property conveyancing may only be perfected by means of a separate notarial deed.

The Contract of Sale

Although it is not legally necessary to record the sale in a written document, a formal contract is almost always drawn up because it is preferable to provide a clear identification of the assets transferred and of the guarantees given by the seller. In addition if future part payments of the purchase price are secured by a charge ("privilège") over the "fonds de commerce", a written contract is required for the validity of this "privilège".

Where a contract of sale is drawn up it must contain certain minimal information prescribed by law: the name of the previous seller (if any), the date and type of the contract of sale, the purchase price, a list of the existing charges, the turnover and profit in respect of the preceding three years, the date and duration of the lease (if any) and the name and address of the landlord or assignor where applicable (see Article 12, Law of 29th June 1935).

Failure to include any of the above information renders the contract of sale voidable at the sole option of the purchaser. Incorrect information exposes the vendor to repayment of the full purchase price in exchange for the transfer back of the "fonds de commerce" to the original owner provided the purchaser brings an action in the courts within one year of the effective date of the sale (Article 13, Law of 29th June 1935).

The provisions referred to above apply to any document, irrespective of its form or avowed purpose, which permits or implements the transfer of a "fonds de commerce". They are applicable in particular to reciprocal put and call options relating to a "fonds de commerce" ("promesse synallagmatique") and to certain call options ("promesse unilatérale de vente") providing for a substantial cancellation fee. They are also applicable to sales subject to a condition precedent.

In practice the execution of the contract of sale is frequently preceded by another (usually shorter) document (e.g. "protocole d'accord", memorandum of understanding, "promesse de vente" combined with a purchase option) which, depending on the precise terms of this pre-contract, may contain a "promesse synallagmatique de vente et d'achat" (where both parties are committed) or a "promesse unilatérale de vente" (where the vendor alone is committed). In the latter case it should be noted that the commitment is void if the document is not registered with the local tax office within 10 days (Article 1840–A of the French Tax Code). A fixed registration tax is payable at this stage (currently FF 500).

Guarantees

The sale of a "fonds de commerce", in addition to specific legislation regulating particular aspects of such transactions, is subject to the general French law of sales (Articles 1582 to 1657 of the Civil Code), which contains a number of provisions relating to guarantees (Articles 1625 to 1649 of the Civil Code). These include a guarantee of title ("garantie d'éviction") and a guarantee against latent defects ("garantie des vices cachés"). The latter provision gives rise in practice to the greatest number of claims and French law, together with the case law relating to it, will be briefly summarised before its application to a "fonds de commerce" is considered.

A latent defect is one which is not readily apparent to an ordinary layman (although, under certain circumstances, the courts will take into account the professional and technical capacity of the purchaser in order to assess whether, in the light of the nature of the latent defect, a professional purchaser should have detected it) at the time of the sale and which, when revealed subsequently, seriously impedes the normal use of the object sold. The manifestation of a latent defect entitles the purchaser, at his sole option, either to a reduction of the purchase price *a posteriori* or to a rescission of the sale. The courts have discretion in their assessment of the existence of a latent defect and as to the extent of the loss suffered by the purchaser. Action must be brought within an (unspecified) short period of time from the date of discovery of the defect (which the courts will determine on a case-by-case basis), failing which the action is rejected or becomes time-barred. It is lawful to provide contractually for a more restricted or more extensive guarantee, although restrictive clauses are valid only where they occur in a contract between parties who are professionals in the same field or specialisation.

Application of the latent defect concept to a "fonds de commerce" raises many difficulties. It has also resulted in abundant case law arising from the fact that the courts have a wide degree of discretion in this regard. The principle is that latent defects are assessed not in relation to the "fonds de commerce" as a whole but in relation to each of the assets which form its constituent parts. Accordingly, while certain circumstances are clear instances of the existence of a "latent defect" (e.g. an infringing trademark or a voidable patent) in the majority of cases the availability of legal protection is uncertain, and in any event dependent on the outcome of time-consuming court proceedings.

In practice the parties rely on contractually agreed representations and warranties which, although they do not remove altogether the need for court resolution of disputes, at least tend to confine the issue to one of interpretation of a clause. The practice of warranty clauses is not as widespread in France as it is elsewhere because of the continental preference for brevity in drafting and the greater reliance placed on judicial solutions. However increasing exposure to cross-border deals has brought about wider acceptance of such internationally used drafting standards and methods. Nevertheless these are not always appropriate for the transfer of a "fonds de commerce", where the purchaser only acquires certain assets and where liabilities are in principle excluded unless agreed otherwise between the parties.

Contracts and Receivables

Contractual rights and obligations are not included in the French concept of "fonds de commerce" and are therefore not transferred when a "fonds de commerce" is sold. There are only three exceptions to this rule provided by specific legislation: contracts of employment (Article L.122–12 of the Labour Code), insurance contracts (Article L.121–10 of the Insurance Code) and publishing contracts (Article 62 of French copyright law). Leases relating to premises where the activity is carried out are part of the "fonds de commerce" and are automatically transferred.

Other types of contract cannot be transferred unless they are specifically listed in the contract of sale: this applies *inter alia* to equipment and financial leases, loans and guarantees, distribution and agency contracts, franchises and contracts for the sale or supply of goods.

While transfer as between seller and purchaser is perfected by the execution of the contract of sale, the transfer is not valid and enforceable against the other contracting parties and third parties in general (e.g. creditors) unless the consent of such other contracting parties has been obtained (usually by letter). Legal writers (and many practitioners) tend to consider that mere notification by letter to the other contracting parties should be sufficient, but this view is not well founded on any law or court decision.

As regards receivables, consent of the seller's debtor is not required for the transfer to be valid. However the transfer is not valid as against the debtor and third parties until notice thereof has been formally served on the debtor by a process-server ("huissier") (Article 1690 of the Civil Code).

Undisclosed Liabilities and Protection of Creditors

In order to inform creditors of the seller (who may or may not have a charge on the "fonds de commerce") that the "fonds de commerce" has been sold, French law provides that the sale must be published within 15 days in a local legal gazette, and within a further 15-day period in a centralised legal publication, the *Bulletin Officiel des Annonces Civiles et Commerciales* (Article 3 of the Law of 17th March 1909). If creditors make themselves known to the vendor (or his designated agent) within the following 10 days, they are entitled to be paid immediately out of the proceeds of sale, provided the vendor recognises the debt (or a court declares the amount to be due, in case of dispute). In this connection the purchase price is almost always (but this is not compulsory) deposited with an escrow agent, who is then responsible for the receipt of creditors' declarations and for payment of amounts due. At all events the purchase price must not be paid to the vendor before the necessary announcements have been made, and the appropriate time periods have expired: otherwise the purchaser would be liable to the vendor's creditors up to the full amount of the purchase price.

If the price is not sufficient to pay off all creditors, any creditor may, within 20 days of the last published announcement in a legal gazette, make a formal offer to purchase the "fonds de commerce" at a price which must be higher by at least one-sixth than the price paid to the vendor. A public auction is then held at which the "fonds de commerce" is adjudicated (Article 5 of the Law of 17th March 1909).

"Location Gérance"

The "location gérance" agreement is a very specific French agreement regulated by the law of 20th March 1956, whereby the owner of a "fonds de commerce" leases it to a third party who carries on the business at his own risk and expense. The lessor remains the owner of the assets constituting the "fonds de commerce" (tangible and intangible assets). Receivables and payables remain in the name of the lessor.

Two prior conditions for entering into a "location gérance" agreement must be met:

- the lessor must have been registered at the Trade and Companies Registry for at least seven years as a merchant; and
- the business in question must have been operated personally by the lessor for a minimum period of 2 years.

However, these two conditions can be waived by virtue of a special court decision at the request of the lessor.

Subject to the precise terms of the "location gérante" agreement, the lessor transfers the responsibilities of running the business to the lessee who assumes the risk of incurring a loss, or the opportunity of making a profit. In exchange for the right to run the business, the lessee pays the lessor an appropriate royalty which can be either fixed or proportional to the turnover. The lessor's charges will mainly consist of depreciation.

Insofar as the arrangement is at "arm's length", the royalty is deductible for tax purposes by the lessee and is considered as a aprofit to the lessor.

The agreement must be concluded for a fixed period which is renewable and the agreement must be published in a legal gazette within the 15 days following its execution. The parties are free to determine their respective rights and obligations as well as the terms and conditions on which the agreement may be terminated. The lessor must continue to pay the lease rentals related to the premises where the business is operated, since this type of lease is not transferred under the "location gérance".

During the six months following the announcement in a legal gazette, the lessor is jointly and severally liable with the lessee for the debts the latter has incurred in operating the "fonds de commerce". Furthermore, the lessor remains jointly liable with the lessee during the whole term of the "location gérance" for the payment of all corporate taxes incurred in operating the business.

Unless otherwise provided by the "location gérance" agreement, the lessee is free to decide whether to continue or discontinue the agreements related to the "fonds de commerce", such as distribution agreements and insurance agreements. However the employment contracts must be taken over in accordance with Article L.122–12 of the Labour Code (see p.113 *et seq.*). Inventories are generally sold by the lessor to the lessee simultaneously with execution of the "location gérance" agreement.

The "location-gérance" of a "fonds de commerce" may be used as a test period to enable potential investors to get accustomed to the business prior to purchasing it.

In cases of deadlock between the investors, or if one of the investors wishes to withdraw, the "location-gérance" agreement can easily be terminated provided there is a clause providing for termination.

From a tax viewpoint, the "location-gérance" method is neutral and does not involve any immediate taxation as it is not considered as a cessation of business. It should nevertheless only be considered as a temporary solution since it is related to a transfer of the running of a "fonds de commerce" and not to a transfer of the business itself.

Merger Transactions

Under French company law, there are three types of merger transaction: "fusion", "scission" and "apport partiel d'actif". A "fusion" is either a "fusion-absorption" where a company completely absorbs another company (merger by amalgamation) or a "fusion-création" where two companies merge to form a new company (merger by consolidation). In both cases the shareholders of the absorbed company receive shares of the absorbing company. A "scission" is a transaction by which all the assets and liabilities of a company are contributed to newly created companies. The shareholders of the contributing company receive shares of all the receiving companies. An "apport partiel d'actif" (or spin-off) is a transfer of part of the assets, with or without liabilities, of a company to another company in exchange for shares of the receiving company. The rules applicable to the "apport partiel d'actif" will be reviewed on p.56 *et seq.*

"Fusion" and "Scission"

The "fusion" and the "scission" are governed by the rules contained in Articles 371 to 389 of the French Company Law and in Articles 254 to 265 of the relevant implementing decree of 23rd March 1967. For this reason, references to "fusion" in this section must always be regarded as including "scission", although the "scission" is infrequent in France because of an unfavourable tax regime for such transactions and because of the difficulty in obtaining the necessary "agrément" of the French Ministry of Economy and Finance.

General Characteristics of a "Fusion"

A "fusion" entails the transfer of all the assets and liabilities of the absorbed company to and for the benefit of the absorbing company. The absorbing company will have title to all the assets of the acquired company and will also assume all its liabilities.

Since all its assets and liabilities are transferred, the acquired company must be wound up. The shareholders of the absorbed company will then receive shares of the absorbing company issued by way of an increase of the latter's share capital, the amount of such increase to be no higher than the net asset value of the absorbed company. The absorbing company may also offer cash provided the amount offered does not exceed 10% of the total value of the shares issued. Non-compliance with this rule will entail disqualification of the transaction as a "fusion" and its treatment as a sale of assets.

If the absorbing company owns shares in the absorbed company, it cannot receive its own shares in exchange and must accordingly limit the increase of its share capital by an amount sufficient to permit the issue of new shares to all shareholders of the absorbed company other than itself. Similarly, if the absorbed company owns some of its own shares, no shares of the absorbing company may be issued in exchange for these shares.

Valuation of the Companies

In practice a financial audit generally carried out by a firm of auditors or accountants. Various methods of valuation are available to determine the value of the absorbing and of the absorbed company. The COB (see p.73 *et seq.*) recommends that several assessments should be made using different methods, the final value being established by way of comparison. The value of each company will then be divided by the relevant number of shares in order to arrive at the value per share.

Where the value of the shares of the absorbing company exceeds their par value, a premium will be created and entered into a special account ("prime de fusion") on its balance sheet. The shareholders, acting upon the proposal of the management of the company, may decide to use this account either to pay for expenses incurred by the company in connection with the transaction or to charge it to a reserve account.

Draft Merger Agreement "Projet de Fusion"

The management (board of directors in a "société anonyme" and "gérant" in a "société à responsabilité limitée) of each of the companies involved are jointly responsible for preparing the draft merger agreement, which must as a matter of law contain the following mandatory information: the form, name and registered office of all the companies involved in the "fusion"; the purpose, aims and conditions of the "fusion"; the dates on which the companies will close their accounts for the purpose of fixing the terms and conditions of the transaction; the effective date of the "fusion" for accounting purposes (the "fusion" is usually implemented with retroactive effect to the closing dates referred to above); a description of the assets and liabilities transferred and their value; the exchange ratio used for the transfers of the shares concerned the amount of the premium; the date of transfer of the shares. The draft merger agreement must be approved by the management of each company and signed by the president (or "gérant" in the case of a SARL) of each of them.

The agreement is then filed with the Trade and Companies Registry and a summary of the mandatory information which it contains must be published in a legal gazette. When one or both of the companies is a publicly held company, a notice must also be published in a special bulletin (BALO) and if the company is listed, the same notice must be inserted in a national financial gazette. These formalities must be complied with at the latest one month before the date of the extraordinary general meeting of shareholders convened to vote on the transaction.

Official Valuation and Shareholders' Approval

A "commissaire aux apports" (official valuer) must be appointed by the Commercial Court at the request of the management of the request of the management of the absorbing company. The "commissaire aux apports" will draft a report containing his valuation of the asset contribution and confirming that the net assets contributed are at least equal to the amount of the capital increase to be resolved by the shareholders as a result of such contribution. This report must be filed with the Trade and Companies Registry and made available to the shareholders at the registered office at least eight days prior to the date of the extraordinary general meeting of the shareholders.

In addition, a "commissaire à la fusion" (merger controller), appointed by the commercial court at the request of either company or jointly by all the companies involved, must check that the value per share of the respective companies is appropriate and that the exchange ratio is fair. The report of the "commissaire à la fusion" will also indicate the method of valuation used, the validity of this method, the resulting values, and any specific problems encountered. This report must be made available to the shareholders of all the companies involved and filed with the Trade and Companies Registry at least one month prior to the date of the extraordinary shareholders' meetings of both companies.

The management of each company must also draft a report which must be made available to the shareholders prior to the extraordinary shareholders' meeting called to vote on the "fusion". In addition to providing information similar to that contained in the report of the "commissaire à la fusion", the management's report must indicate the economic and legal reasons for the "fusion".

Shareholders of both the absorbing and the absorbed company will vote on the "fusion" by a resolution passed by a qualified majority (two-thirds of the voting rights in an SA or an SCA and three-quarters of the shares of a SARL).

Where the absorbing company owns 100% of the share capital of the absorbed company, the report of the "commissaire à la fusion", the approval of the "fusion" by an extraordinary shareholders' meeting of the absorbed company and the report of the management are not required.

It should be added that where one of the companies involved has issued different classes of shares, the "fusion" must be submitted for approval to a meeting of each of the special classes of holders.

Consequences of the "Fusion"
The "fusion" will be effective on the following dates

- in the case of creation of one or more new companies, at the date of registration with the Trade and Companies Registry of the last new company; and
- in cases where existing companies only are involved, at the date on which the last shareholders' meeting to be held approved the "fusion". If the "traité de fusion" provides for a different date, this date must not be later than the end of the absorbing company's current fiscal year, and cannot overlap into the absorbed company's current fiscal year.

As a result of the transfer of liabilities entailed by the "fusion", the absorbing company becomes, by operation of law, the debtor of all creditors of the absorbed company in lieu of the latter. Any creditor of the absorbed or of the absorbing company whose claim is prior to the date of publication of the "projet de fusion" may oppose the "fusion" by an action in the commercial courts within 30 days of such publication. This opposition cannot in fact prevent the continuation of the "fusion" operations. The commercial court may reject the opposition. Alternatively it may order the absorbed company to repay these debts or to provide security if the absorbing company so offers and if the security is accepted as sufficient. Failing repayment of the debts or the offer of security as ordered, the "fusion" will not be valid against the said creditor and he will benefit from a preferred right against the creditors of the receiving company in respect of the transferred assets.

Where the absorbed company has issued bonds, other than bonds convertible into or exchangeable for shares, it may decide either to submit the "projet de fusion" to a bondholders' meeting or to repay the bonds. In the first case, the bondholders may reject the "projet de fusion", although such refusal cannot stop the "fusion" operations (except where such refusal is expressed by holders of bonds exchangeable for shares). The bondholders will then have to follow the opposition procedure described above.

"Apport Partiel d'Actif (Spin-off)
An "apport partiel d'actif" is a scheme by which a company transfers part of its business to another company, the consideration being shares issued by the receiving company. The contributing company may either transfer one or more of its assets (such as pemises or an interest in another company) or a set of assets capable of being organised as an independent business (such as a division of a company). In the latter case, the "apport partiel d'actif" may be regarded as a "fusion" or a "scission" as regards the assets transferred. Accordingly, Article 387 of the French Company Law provides that the companies concerned can decide to submit the "apport partiel d'actif" to the rules applicable to "scissions". The COB (see p.73 *et seq.*) strongly recommends the adoption of these rules where the contributing company is a listed company which transfers a significant part of its assets. Where the assets transferred can be regarded as an independent business, the special tax treatment provided for "fusions" and "scissions" is available (see p.109 *et seq.*)

The procedure for the "apport partiel d'actif" is as follows. First, the management of each of the companies involved draft an "apport partiel d'actif" agreement which must indicate each asset and each liability transferred together with their valuation and which usually contains warranties and representations on the part of the contributing company. A "commissaire aux apports" (official valuer) must then be appointed by the commercial court at the request of the management of both companies. The "commissaire aux apports" will draft a report containing his valuation of the assets contributed. This report must be filed with the Trade and Companies Registry and made available to the shareholders of the receiving company at the registered office at least eight days prior to the date of the extraordinary shareholders' meeting. Finally the shareholders of the receiving company will be asked to vote on the "apport partiel d'actif" and to increase the capital by an amount equal to the approved contribution: the relevant resolution must be passed by a qualified majority (two-thirds in an SA or in an SCA, three-quarters in a SARL).

When the partial contribution covers all the assets, liabilities, rights and obligations of a business, a contribution with retroactive effect is from a practical viewpoint almost mandatory; in fact the assets contributed, as identified and valued in the draft agreement, must still exist at the date the resolution is passed if no retroactive effect was provided for. In practice, of course, this is impossible, especially in the case of inventories.

Share Acquisitions

Instead of acquiring the assets of a company by means of a sale of the "fonds de commerce" or a merger ("fusion" or "apport partiel d'actif"), a potential acquirer may seek to obtain control through an acquisition of the shares of the company owning the assets. Preference for this solution may derive from the fact that share acquisitions are simpler (at least for unquoted companies) and in certain cases more effective from a tax viewpoint (this is certainly the case when compared to the sale of a "fonds de commerce").

Control

While the percentage of shares acquired does not have any impact on the structure and procedure for implementing the transaction (except in the case of quoted companies), it does have significant consequences with regard to control of the target company. As there are several statutory definitions of control, each of which applies to specific circumstances, control in practice means the ability to run the company without hindrance, whether at management level or by means of shareholders' resolutions.

Control in the Shareholders' Meetings

In the most common types of commercial company (e.g. the SA and the SARL) management is appointed and annual accounts approved by a shareholders' resolution passed by a simple majority as referred to above (see p.10 *et seq.*). The ability to command 50% of the votes either by direct ownership of the relevant shares or through contractual arrangements with other shareholders (see pp.39 to 40 *et seq.* above) results in this respect in the exercise of financial control by one or a group of shareholders. Furthermore, as there are various types of securities which may be issued by SAs or SCAs, control is assessed in such companies on the voting rights (in order to take into account double voting rights, voting certificates and stock options granted to employees under stock option plans) instead of on the shares. Absolute control of a company entails the ability to pass extraordinary resolutions by a majority of two-thirds of the voting rights in an SA and three-quarters of the shares in a SARL.

Control at the Management Level

In an SA control of the board of directors is also necessary since the "president directeur général" (president and managing director) is appointed by a board resolution passed by a simple majority. Control at the management level therefore requires that the acquirer is represented by nominees representing more than half the number of Directors on the board. In a SARL management consists of a single "gérant" who is appointed by an ordinary resolution of the shareholders. As regards the other types of company ("sociétés de personnes"), special attention should be drawn to the articles of association which in principle have flexibility to determine the organisation of the corporate management in terms of quorum and majority required to pass resolutions. With respect to the SCS or the SCA, control of the management is a key issue as management is in essence independent from the shareholding (see p.10 *et seq.* above). These considerations should be borne in mind when the structure of the transaction is being negotiated.

Control and Related Consequences with Respect to the Acquisition
In addition to the control over the management and the resolutions passed at the shareholders' meetings, the issue of whether a potential purchaser acquires control of a company or not results in significant practical effects.

Application of Specific Regulations Governing the Sale of a "Fonds de Commerce"
Pursuant to Law No. 70–9 of 2nd January 1970 governing implementation of the sale, purchase or lease of a "fonds de commerce" or real property, any intermediary, especially any agent, in charge of the sale of a "fonds de commerce" or real property must hold a special power of attorney as well as a professional card in order to carry out its activities. Under article 1 of Law No. 70–9, the statutory provisions apply to any individual or entity which carries out in the ordinary course of its business intermediary transactions with respect to the purchase or sale of non-negotiable shares of a company with underlying assets including a real property or a "fonds de commerce".

On the basis of Article 1, the acquisition of control of a SARL falls within the scope of Law No. 70–9, unlike the acquisition of control of an SA or SCA, as the shares of these companies are freely negotiable. Despite these clear provisions, the "Cour de Cassation" has held that the sale of the whole of the share capital of a company running a "fonds de commerce", irrespective of its corporate legal form, falls within the scope of Law No. 70–9, as the transfer of shares is necessarily related to the transfer of the underlying "fonds de commerce". Although this decision was criticised, it follows therefrom that any company acting as an intermediary in the sale of corporate control (whether in a SARL, SA or SCA) should hold a professional card as well as a special power of attorney in order to exercise its functions.

Tax Consequences

It should be noted that until recently the acquisition of all the shares of a company was considered by the tax authorities as the sale of the underlying "fonds de commerce" and taxed accordingly at the rate of 14.2% on the value of the assets transferred (see the tax regime described at p.104 *et seq.*) However the Cour de Cassation issued significant decisions in 1984 which ruled against the doctrine of the tax administration on the basis that the transaction remains a purchase of shares and does not result in the creation of a new legal entity. Since then, the tax administration has reversed its previous rulings regarding the taxation of the shares as the sale of a "fonds de commerce" and has declared that it will no longer disqualify such transactions unless the companies involved are wound up and replaced by a newly created company. Accordingly, a sale of all of the shares is subject to the standard registration tax of 4.80% in the case of sales of shares of an SARL or "société de personnes" and to a registration tax of 1%, with a maximum ceiling of FF 20,000, in the case of sales of shares of an SA or SCA (see p.109 *et seq.*).

Commercial Nature of the Transaction

Although the purchase of shares is in principle considered as a civil transaction, it becomes commercial if the transaction results in the purchaser acquiring control of the company concerned. Accordingly, the stock purchase agreement can validly provide for an arbitration clause and the rules governing evidence and prescription in commercial transactions are more flexible (evidence may be adduced by all means and prescription is extended to ten years); the sellers are jointly liable, unless expressly provided otherwise, in the event that they issued warranties in favour of the purchaser.

Unquoted Companies

Structure of the Transaction

There are usually three stages involved in implementing a transaction. The first is the exchange of a preliminary document (memorandum of understanding, letter of intent, etc.) which contains the principal features of the transaction and which may be legally binding, depending on whether the parties have committed to buy and sell the shares respectively. The document often provides for the possibility of audits (accounting, tax and legal) and sets a date for the final closing following the fulfilment of certain conditions precedent. These may include obtaining necessary regulatory authorisations (for non-French investors) or shareholders' approval for the transfer of the shares (when such approval is required by the articles of association) or the confirmation, by the audits to be carried out, of the accuracy of the information supplied by the seller on the company.

Where both parties are committed and there is no condition precedent to be fulfilled, the agreement should technically be regarded as a sale with the consequence that registration tax on the purchase price should in principle be paid at the time (see p.109 *et seq.*).

In most share acquisition transactions, the purchase price paid by the purchaser is far above the nominal value of the shares of the target company. Pursuant to Article 1591 of the Civil Code and pursuant to French case law, the purchase price in the contract of sale must be determined by the parties or at least determinable on the basis of the provisions of the sale agreement itself and without the necessity for a further agreement between the parties subsequent to the transfer of the shares; failure to comply with this requirement results in the sale contract being null and void.

The sale agreement must therefore (a) either determine the purchase price prior to the transfer of the shares, or (b) include an objective formula on the basis of which the purchase price can be automatically determined, or alternatively (c) provide for recourse to a third party pursuant to Article 1592 of the Civil Code, which provides that "the determination of the purchase price may be left to the arbitration of a third party; if the third party is unwilling or unable to make the estimate, there is no sale".

Where the parties leave the determination to the decision of an independent expert(s) under Article 1592 of the Civil Code, the parties must either designate the expert(s) prior to the transfer of the shares (the expert(s) frequently being selected from among the professionals responsible for the financial audit of the company) or must provide in the sale agreement for the expert to be appointed by a designated tribunal where the parties cannot agree on the choice of expert (s). Failure to provide expressly as aforesaid renders the sale agreement null and void for uncertainty of the purchase price. The provisions concerning the purchase price should accordingly be drafted with care.

Documentation — Warranty Provisions

Once the preliminary audits and the other conditions precedent have been completed a full agreement should normally be drawn up and signed by both parties. The greater part of this document will consist of the declarations and warranties and indemnity provisions.

Statutory Warranty Provisions

Unlike the purchase of a "fonds de commerce", the acquisition of shares brings with it a portion of the liabilities as well as the corporate assets. As a result the purchaser always tries as far as possible to supplement the warranty provisions of the Civil Code by contractual warranty provisions.

The negotiation of adequate warranty provisions is crucial

since in the absence of such clauses only the Civil Code provisions relating to guarantees (Articles 1625 to 1649) would apply (see p.45 *et seq.* above). However protection under these articles is limited in practice, since the courts have held that the guarantee against latent defects applies only to the shares themselves and not to the assets owned by the company. Legal protection is therefore much more restricted in the case of a sale of shares than in the case of a sale of a "fonds de commerce".

Another application of the statutory protection is the ability for the purchaser, on the basis of Article 1116 of the Civil Code, to seek a judgment rendering the sale of shares null and void if he can prove that his consent was vitiated because of wilful misrepresentation ("dol"). It must be borne in mind that evidence of wilful misrepresentation is admitted only on the strictest terms by French courts. An action for wilful misrepresentation will only succeed if all the following conditions are satisfied:

- the existence of positive acts or (in certain cases) omissions on the part of the seller aimed at misleading the buyer (such as the production of forged documents, lies or withholding of information);
- the existence of a clear intention to mislead the buyer;
- the buyer must have relied on the action of the seller to consent to the transaction;
- the mistake of the buyer must be legitimate taking account of the level of his professional expertise.

If all the above conditions are met and if the buyer does not intend to render the sale null and void, he may start an action in tort against the seller.

Contractual Warranty Provisions

As a result of the case law referred to above and the limited effects of the statutory warranties, the contractual warranty provisions are drafted in great detail. Although the contractual warranty provisions are designated under the general term of "garantie de passif", this term covers in practice various types of warranty which result in different commitments for the issuer. A broad distinction should be drawn between:

- The strict "garantie de passif" where the seller who guarantees the purchaser under numerous declarations against certain risks deriving from periods prior to completion of the sale or prior to the guaranteed balance sheet (such as accounting, financial, tax, labour law, contractual or environmental risks) undertakes on a direct basis to indemnify the creditors of the company or the company itself.
- The price revision clause, pursuant to which the seller guarantees the net equity of the company sold at the same level as it appears in the guaranteed balance sheet. In that case, if the guarantee is called, the seller indemnifies the buyer in respect of any reduction in the net equity of the company pro rata to his former shareholding. It is questionable whether this does not render the purchase price undetermined or undeterminable at the time of the sale agreement (for the reasons set out at p.61 *et seq.* above).

While the strict "garantie de passif" is in some ways more favourable to the purchaser, since the seller's undertaking is for an unlimited amount (unless otherwise provided), the price revision clause is to be recommended to the seller since (a) his payment undertaking may not in any case exceed the purchase price paid by the purchaser even if the liabilities prove subsequently to be higher and (b) being a guarantee of net equity all plusses and minuses are set off against each other.

- A full assets and liabilities guarantee where the seller guarantees, on a line-by-line basis, the assets and liabilities of the guaranteed balance sheet.

It should be emphasised that facts regarding the company which may have been disclosed to the potential purchaser in the course of the audits conducted prior to the acquisition, in particular facts which may have given rise to the constitution of reserves, are often excluded from the scope of the indemnification clause.

Closing of the Transaction
Closing requires the execution of a document of transfer and compliance with certain formalities designed to perfect the transfer. In addition a meeting of the shareholders' or of the board of directors' must in certain cases be held to authorise the transfer or to approve the transferee as a new shareholder.

Legal Formalities
Transfer documents and formalities are not the same in the case of an SA as they are for a SARL. In an SA or SCA the vendor must complete and sign a share transfer form ("ordre de mouvement") which is then delivered to the purchaser, and by the latter to the issuing company. Upon receipt of this document the company must make the appropriate change in its register of shareholders, enter the transfer in its transfer register and issue to the purchaser a document certifying that he is now the owner of the shares transferred ("attestation d'inscription"). Although French company law does not contain any clear indication in this respect, legal writers generally agree that a transfer of shares is perfected at the date on which it is entered in the register of shareholders. The transfer is perfected as between the parties at the date on which consent to the transaction is expressed: this will usually take place on the closing date (when all the conditions precedent have been fulfilled) although from a legal point of view the relevant transfer date may sometimes take place prior to the closing date when the parties have agreed upon the object and the price of the sale. In fact, pursuant to Article 1589 of the Civil Code, a commitment to purchase is valid and legally binding when the parties have agreed on the underlying object of the sale and on the price.

In the case of a SARL or of a "société de personnes", the transfer of shares which are not negotiable must comply with a cumbersome procedure: the transfer must be recorded in a written agreement and the sale is valid as against the company at the date on which this agreement is officially delivered at the registered office of the company against a receipt signed by the "gérant", or at the date on which notice of the sale is officially served on the company, with a copy of the agreement, by a "huissier" (process-server). The transfer is valid as against third parties only when copies of the agreement have been officially filed with the Trade and Companies Registry.

Board and Shareholder Approvals

Where control of a company has been acquired, it will be necessary to hold a meeting of the shareholders to appoint the purchaser's representatives as directors on the board (or the purchaser's nominees as "gérant" in the case of a SARL or "société de personnes"). In the case of an SA it may also be necessary to hold a meeting of the board of directors to appoint the new "président directeur général" of the company (see p.57 *et seq.* above).

In the case of a SARL, French company law provides that the shares cannot be sold to a person who is not already a shareholder unless the proposed purchase has been vetted by an extraordinary resolution of the shareholders passed by a majority of three-quarters. The proposed purchase must be notified in advance to the company and to each of the shareholders: failure to reply within three months of such notification is regarded as implicit consent. If the company refuses to approve the proposed sale, the other shareholders or the company itself must acquire or cause the shares to be acquired within three months from the date of such refusal. The above provisions are mandatory and cannot be contracted out of.

There is no comparable compulsory procedure in the case of an SA. However the articles of association may lawfully contain a provision subjecting sales to a third party to the prior authorisation of the board of directors or of the general meeting of shareholders (see p.10 *et seq.* above). Where there is such a provision, the procedure to be followed in relation to a proposed sale of shares is identical to that outlined above for a SARL. If the shares are quoted, each of the three-month periods referred to above is reduced to 30 market days.

Finally, where a parent company sells the whole of its interest in a subsidiary which represents a substantial part of its business, the courts could regard this as an implied change of activity entailing an amendment to the objects clause of the company. Any such amendment should of course be authorised by an extraordinary resolution of the shareholders passed by a two-thirds majority in an SA or an SCA (with the consent of the "commandités") and by a three-quarters majority in a SARL. Failure to obtain such authorisation may subsequently result in the transaction being invalidated by the court. It is therefore prudent, in borderline cases, to obtain the authorisation of the shareholders in order to avoid any subsequent difficulties.

Leveraged buy-out ("Rachat d'une Entreprise par ses Salariés" or "RES"

The techniques of the leveraged buy-out (LBO) has been successfully used in France as elsewhere and its adaptation to the French legal context does not raise major difficulties. The LBO was governed by the law of 17th June 1987. This expired on 31st December 1991 since the tax incentives granted under the 1987 law were only temporary. The new regime which replaces the previous law as from 1st January 1992 and which is intended to expire on 31st December 1996, is less attractive from a tax viewpoint, as will be seen below.

Qualifying Conditions

The qualifying conditions regarding the target company are that:

- the target company must be subject to the standard corporate income tax and must carry out industrial, commercial, professional or agricultural activities;
- the employees of the target company holding shares in the holding company must be at least five and must represent a minimum of 10% of the total employees of the target company under 500 employees and 5% of the total employees above this threshold.

The qualifying conditions regarding the holding company are that:

- the holding company must be a new company with a corporate purpose exclusively dedicated to the purchase and holding of shares in the target company;
- the employees of the target company or of any of its subsidiaries (being companies in which the target company holds a minimum 50% shareholding) including the president of the board of directors, the general managers, the president of the directorate or the "gérants" (if their remuneration is treated as salary income for tax purposes) must together hold more than one-third of the voting rights of the new holding company. In this respect one must take into account shares issued with double voting rights, the potential voting rights which may arise from the conversion of bonds or from the exercise of subscription rights and the indirect shareholding resulting from the creation by the employees of a special-purpose "société civile" or from a "fonds commun de placement d'entreprise" (special investment fund) holding only the employees' shareholdings in the holding company.

When these prior conditions are met, the holding company must purchase within the two months following its registration more than 50% of the voting rights of the target company for a purchase price determined on normal arm's length terms and which are not obviously excessive. If the employees directly own shares of the target company, they must contribute their shareholding to the holding company in order to qualify for the favourable RES tax regime.

Tax Advantages Related to the RES Regime

A number of tax advantages are granted to the employees initiating the RES. Such employees can either:

- deduct from their gross salary received from the target company the financial charges payable in respect of borrowings contracted by them to finance their cash subscriptions to the share capital of the holding company, up to a maximum amount of FF 100,000 per year over a five-year period; or
- enjoy an income tax reduction for an amount representing 25% of the payments for cash subscriptions made over a three-year period following the creation of the holding company, up to a maximum of FF 40,000 (for single persons) and FF 80,000 for a married couple.

Any employee holding directly or indirectly at least 50% of the voting rights of the holding company or target company is not eligible for the RES tax regime.

The above tax advantages (i.e. deduction of financial charges or reduction of income tax) remain subject to the holding by the employees of their shareholding in the holding company or in the special purpose "société civile" or investment fund for a minimum five-year period.

Tax advantages are also granted to the holding company. The purchase by the holding company of the shareholding in the target company on the conditions referred to above is exempt from any registration tax, even if evidenced by a deed in writing.

Despite the success of the RES technique, two potential dangers must be avoided in this type of transaction. It is frequently the case that lending banks require the benefit of securities on the target company's assets. This is not possible in France: Article 217–9 of the French Company Law prohibits the creation of securities by a company over its own assets to guarantee the acquisition of its own shares by a third party. In addition the management of the target company could be charged with misuse of the company's assets ("abus de biens sociaux"). This is a criminal offence punishable by a fine of FF 2000 to FF 2,500,000 and/or up to five years' imprisonment. The courts tend to treat such transactions rather more leniently when they occur between parent and subsidiary or between affiliated companies provided (a) those companies belong to a *bona fide* group; (b) the transaction benefits the group as a whole; and (c) there is adequate consideration. Notwithstanding this favourable case law, great care should be exercised when implementing a transaction of this type.

Dividend distributions by the target company after the RES has been completed, which are used to fund debt repayments made by the holding company, can in certain cases prove to be against the company's interests on the basis that there sums might well be put to a more beneficial use given the situation of the company. If a distribution is nonetheless decided by the majority shareholder(s), the minority shareholder(s) can apply to the court for an order cancelling this decision and the attendant dividend distribution on the grounds that the majority has misused its voting power ("abus de majorité").

The RES remains a popular technique of acquisition because of the favourable tax treatment granted to employees, in particular the deductibility of financing charges sustained by the employees in connection with the acquisition or the reduction of income tax. However the tax credit which was granted under the Law of 17th June 1987 to the special purpose company holding the shares of the target company has been removed in the 1992 Finance Law. As a consequence, the opportunity to offset the profits of the target company against the losses of the holding company which result from the indebtedness of the latter, simply disappears. The easiest opportunity to offset results to the holding company and the target company applies when companies hold at least 95% of the share capital of the target company, under the tax consolidation regime (see p.100 below).

Quoted Companies

The acquisition of a controlling interest in a quoted company may be effected only through the procedure of the "offre publique" (takeover bid) with the possibility in certain cases of using a simplified procedure ("offre publique simplifiée").

By way of introduction, shares listed on the Stock Exchange can be traded on three different markets:

- the official market ("cote officielle"), which is subdivided into the "marché à rèlement mensuel" where payment of the transactions occurs once a month on the settlement date and the "marché au comptant" where payment occurs simultaneously with the transaction. Companies are required to offer a minimum of 25% of their shares to the public on this market;
- the second market ("second marché") where companies are only required to offer 10% of their shares to the public;
- the over-the-counter market ("hors cote") where the company or any shareholder may require registration of the company.

Regulatory Overview

The sale of shares quoted on the official and on the second market must be carried out through a "sociéte de bourse" (brokerage house). The "sociétés de bourse" exercise a monopoly with respect to the sale of quoted shares purusant to

Article 1, Subsection 3 of the Law of 22nd January 1989 except in the case of sale:

- between two individuals;
- between two companies, one of which holds more than 20% of the share capital of the other;
- between a legal entity other than a company and a company held as to not less than 20% by the legal entity in question;
- between insurance companies of the same group;
- between legal entities and pension funds managed by such legal entities;

Furthermore, there is no obligation to act through a "société de bourse" (and hence to pay the stock exchange transfer tax see p.109 *et seq.*) when a sale of shares quoted on the French stock exchange takes place outside France between two non-French companies.

Failure to comply with the monopoly situation described above would render the sale of shares void and would result in the payment by the seller of a fine equal to twice the value of the shares concerned. In relation to sales of shares quoted over-the-counter, the obligation to act through a "société de bourse" remains disputable.

The essential rules governing the purchase of shares in a quoted company are contained in:

- the Law dated 2nd August 1989 relating to the security and transparency of the financial Stock Market (Title II and more especially Articles 14 and 15) which has addressed this issue for the first time;
- the "Réglement Général" issued by the "Conseil des Bourses de Valeur" (CBV) on 28th September 1989, as amended on 15th May 1992;
- the "Réglement" 89–03 dated 28th September 1989 of the "Commission des Opérations de Bourse" (COB).

Supervisory Authorities

The regulations referred to above are issued by the following three Stock Exchange Authorities, which are also charged with supervising their enforcement.

The COB

The COB, which is comparable to the American SEC, is an administrative body (but not a legal entity) with a president appointed for a six-year term by a decree issued by the Council of Ministers and a college of eight members which meets at least twice a month upon request of the president.

The COB is essentially responsible for:

- the protection of savings invested in securities or in any other public investments; the COB accordingly gives clearance for the appointment of the managers of investment funds (for "sociétés d'investissement à variable" or SICAVs —), for the establishment of "sociétés de gestion de portefeuilles individuels" (individual portfolio management companies) or for the publication of "notes d'information" in the context of a takeover bid (see p.77 *et seq.* below).
- ensuring the provision of information to investors; and
- supervising the fair operation of the markets for securities, quoted financial products or negotiable forward contracts.

The COB may propose to the government the modification of laws or regulations. It may also issue regulations (among which the "Réglement" 89–03) recommendations, instructions or rulings ("rescrit") and it has powers of investigation in respect of any activities which might be connected with criminal violations, such as insider dealing (see p.91 *et seq.*).

In order to enforce these powers, the COB may impose sanctions such as injunctions or fines; it may also require the prosecutor of the court ("parquet") to impose criminal penalties or to grant provisional injunctions against an infringing party, although it is not entitled to cause the prosecutor to initiate criminal proceedings.

The CBV

The conseil des Bourses de Valeurs (CBV) is a professional body, which is related to Stock Exchange activities in France, working under the supervision of the Ministry of Economy and Finance. The CBV sets out a "Réglement Général" (General Regulation) approved by the Ministry of Economy and Finance after the COB and the Banque de France have given an advice with respect thereto. The purpose of the "Réglement Général" is to determine *inter alia*:

- the rules regarding operation of the Stock Exchange market, suspension of quotations and takeover bids;
- the rules regarding registration of securities on the official market or second market, their trading and delisting. It should be noted that the COB may veto CBV decisions relating to the registration or delisting of securities on the Stock Exchange.

The CBV is also the entity responsible for giving clearance to the new "sociétés de bourse" (brokerage houses) and for excercising disciplinary authority over this profession. Any decision of the CBV must be adequately justified and may be subject to appeal to the Court of Appeals of Paris.

The SBF

The Sociéte de Bourses Françaises (SBF) is a specialised institution which assists the CBV in the review of files submitted to the CBV in relation to the registration or delisting of securities on the Stock Exchange. In addition to its powers in the context of takeover bids (see para. below), the SBF is in charge of the supervision and suspension of quotations of securities on the Stock Exchange.

"Offres Publiques" (OP)
There are two types of takeover bids: the "offre publique d'achat" (OPA), where the consideration is cash and the "offre publique d'échange" (OPE) where the consideration consists of shares of the bidder or a related company. The offer or company may also pay partly in cash and partly in shares, this combination being called an "offre publique mixte" (OPM).

Takeover procedures are closely supervised by the CBV and the COB. This supervision involves prior approval of the OP, the issue of information and notices to the public, monitoring of the target company and monitoring of the takeover transaction itself. The rules summarised below apply too both OPAs and OPEs.

Prior Approval of the CBV
The intended OP must be filed with the CBV by a bank or other financial institution which guarantees the irrevocability and due fulfilment of the undertakings of the company initiating the OP. It must contain the following information:

- the purpose of the OP and the intentions of the offeror at the time of filing;
- the number and characteristics of the shares in the target company already held by the offeror;
- the OP must be made for 100% of the share capital and the voting rights of the target company, whereas prior to May 1992 OP could be made for not less than two-thirds of the voting rights. The rule enacted in May 1992 by the CBV was intended to protect minority shareholders and to maintain equal treatment of all shareholders. Subject to this rule, the offeror may make his offer conditional upon receipt of a stated percentage of shares, failing which the OP may be permitted to lapse. Exceptions to the requirement to offer for 100% of the share capital and the voting rights are limited to:

(a) offers restricted to 10% of the target company's voting rights or share capital, including the offeror's existing shareholdings and voting rights (whether direct or indirect);
(b) redemption offers with a view to cancellation of the shares; and
(c) the purchase of "certificats d'investissement" by a holder of "certificats de droit de vote" or the purchase of "certificats de droit de vote" by a holder of "certificats d'investissement", in which case the offer may be limited to a number of "certificats de droit de vote" or "certificats d'investissement" equal to the number of "certificats d'investissement" or "certificats de droit de vote" already owned by the offeror;

- the price or exchange ratio offered, and the factors taken into consideration for establishing these (the CBV may request the offeror to review the price offered if it considers the price unacceptable on the basis of objective criteria);
- if the OP is initiated by a foreign company, a copy of the application for authorisation or of the prior declaration sent to the French Treasury must be included (see p.31 *et seq.*);
- the period for which the OP will remain open for acceptance, which cannot be less than 20 market days, subject to certain exceptions described below for OPs subject to a simplified procedure.

Upon receipt of the proposal, the SBF must suspend the quotation of the shares of the target company by publication of a notice of suspension of quotation ("avis de suspension de cotation"). In addition, it must inform the Ministry of Economy and Finance (Treasury Department and Competition Council) and the COB of the proposed OP. The officers of the target company must on the same date inform the workers' council of the proposed OP.

The period during which the offeror and the target company must comply with the "Réglement" of the CBV and the "Réglement" of the COB begins on the day of publication of the "avis de suspension", which discloses the principal terms of the OP. When the CBV examines the OP, it may require additional justifications and guarantees and may require the deposit of cash or securities. It must approve or reject the OP within five market days from the date of filing. Its decision is published by the SBF. If the OP is approved, the "avis de recevabilité" published by the SBF must disclose all the terms of the OP.

Public Information

The company initiating the OP must draft a "note d'information" (information notice) containing information on:

- the identity and characteristics of the offeror;
- his intentions over the next 12 months regarding the industrial, financial and labour policy in the target company;
- the price or exchange ratio offered and the factors taken into consideration in establishing these;
- the number of shares which the offeror is undertaking to purchase;
- the number of shares which the offeror already holds in the target company whether directly, indirectly or in concert with third parties;
- the financial terms of the transaction and their impact on the assets, activities and profits of the target company;
- the agreements, if any, with respect to the OP to which the offeror is a party or of which he is aware.

This draft is submitted for approval to the COB at the date on which the "avis de suspension de cotation" is published. The COB must approve or reject the "note d'information" within five market days. The draft must also be submitted to the target company. The "note d'information" has to be communicated to (a) the target company as soon as it is approved by the COB and (b) the shareholders of the target company not later than four market days from its approval by the COB.

The target company must also draft an information notice to be submitted for approval to the COB within the five market days following the date on which the information notice drafted by the offeror was submitted to the COB. This information notice must contain a presentation of the company, a breakdown of its share capital, any shareholders agreement of which the target company is aware, the advice of the board of directors or supervisory board on the benefits or risks of the OP for the target company and for its shareholders. It should be noted that when the OP is amicable, a single information notice may be drafted by both the offeror and the target company.

Processing of the OP

The OP starts with the publication of an "avis d'ouverture" made by the SBF as soon as it is informed of the approval of the "note d'information" by the COB and of any other French regulatory approvals which may be required (see p.31 *et seq.* and p.35 *et seq.*).

The "avis d'ouverture" specifies, in addition to the information already contained in the "avis de suspension", the number of shares which the offeror already holds, the minimum number of shares which must be delivered in response to the OP and the timetable for the OP.

The OP must be irrevocable and must remain open for at least 20 market days from the date of publication of the "avis d'ouverture". The CBV may extend this period by postponing the closing date of the offer. In such case, the SBF publishes the new timetable for the offer. Selling orders given in response to the OP can be cancelled at any time during the period in which the OP remains open.

All selling orders are transmitted by the "sociétés de bourse" (brokers) to the SBF. The result of the OP is then published by the SBF. If the OP has failed, the shares are returned to their owners.

During the offer period of an OP for securities listed on the "marché à réglement mensuel" (monthly market), the negotiation of listed options is suspended. Instructions given on the monthly market must be paid up in full, save when the instructions are the counterpart of positions taken before the publication of the "avis de suspension", or when the transactions are carried out by market-makers under their regulatory functions on the MONEP; the sale of options must be completed by delivery of securities, save when the transactions are carried out by market-makers under their regulatory functions on the MONEP.

There is a basic difference between OPAs and OPEs as regards the ability of the offeror or of parties acting in concert with him to conduct open market purchases during the OP. In an OPE, such persons are prohibited from acquiring shares of the target company, whereas they are allowed to do so in the case of an OPA if the offer is for 100% of the shares (except when the offer is conditional upon receipt of a stated percentage of shares or in certain cases where the OPA is subject to a simplified procedure). However if the price of the shares so purchased is in excess of the offer price of the OP, the offer price of the OP must automatically be increased by 2%.

Competing OPs may be lodged with the CBV until five market days prior to the closing date of the initial OP. The publication of the "avis de suspension" relating to a competing OP annuls all selling orders given in response to the initial OP. The CBV will extend the duration of the initial OP to the date of expiry of the subsequent OP. Competing OPAs must be at an offer price of not less than 102% of the price per share of the initial OP, except where the competing OPA is not conditional upon a minimum number of shares being delivered in response to it (whereas the initial OP was subject to such a condition). As regards competing OPEs, the CBV merely considers whether the modifications brought to the offer are significantly better than the previous terms and whether an extension of the initial timetable is necessary.

The initial offeror must indicate to the CBV his intentions (e.g. whether to maintain or cancel the OP or to modify its terms by a "surenchére") at the latest five market days after the publication of the "avis d'ouverture" of the competing offer.

The CBV may set a time limit for filing the successive competing offers when more than 10 weeks have elapsed since the publication of the "avis d'ouverture" of the initial offer. This time limit may not be less than three market days from the date of publication of the decision rendering each competing offer official.

Between the closing date and the result of the OP, the offeror and persons acting in concert with him may not sell any of the shares received in response to the OP: they may purchase such shares only at a price equal to the offer price of the OP.

Mandatory OP

Any person, whether acting alone or in concert with others, who holds directly or indirectly more than one-third of the voting rights or of the share capital of a quoted company, must file an OP with the CBV for 100% of the share capital and voting rights of the target company. The OP may not be conditional on presentation of a minimum number of shares. Such procedure is not applicable to the purchase of securities listed on the "hors cote" market.

A mandatory OP must also be filed when any person, acting alone or jointly, holds directly or indirectly between one-third and one half of the voting rights or of the share capital of a company and increases such shareholding by more than 2% within a period of less than one year or holds the absolute majority.

The CBV may grant exemptions to this rule in the following cases:

- the one-third threshold is passed as a result of a transfer for nil consideration, a merger, an increase of share capital for cash in favour of specific persons or a partial business transfer;
- the acquisition of shares or voting rights beyond the one-third threshold does not exceed 3% of the total number of shares or voting rights of the company or the purchaser has undertaken to redistribute any purchased shares or voting rights in excess of the 3% limit within period of 18 months;
- the increase in percentage of the total number of shares or voting rights results from the reduction in the total number of shares or voting rights of the company;
- the purchaser controlled the company before passing the one-third threshold. A company "controls" another for this purpose where it in practice determines the exercise of its voting rights, the decision-making process in the general shareholders' meetings;
- the company is already under the majority control of a shareholder acting in concert;
- the purchaser happens to hold more than one-third of its own account by way of purchase from one or several persons outside the group to which it belongs and such a group already controls the company within the framework of consolidated accounting policies;
- the purchasers who control the company redistribute the shares within their group without changing significantly the allocation among the partners in the group;
- the threshold is passed pursuant to an agreement to act in

concert already disclosed to the CBV and published by the SBF and the parties to the agreement have not directly or indirectly, within the year preceding such disclosure, purchased a significant number of shares with voting rights and they undertake that for a period of two years they will not modify significantly the balance of their respective shareholdings within the concert group.

Management of the Target Company

The managers of the target company must conduct its corporate affairs in a prudent manner during the OP, in particular with respect to public comments, stock exchange transactions, and the use of company credit and assets. Any extraordinary decision must be notified to the public subject to the supervision of the COB. In addition, the management of the target company is not permitted to increase any existing cross-ownership percentages.

Supervision of the OP

During the course of the OP, all companies involved including their directors, shareholders holding at least 5% of the share capital or of the voting rights at ordinary shareholders" meetings of the target company, and any other person acting in concert with them, are required to disclose to the SBF, on a daily basis after the market has closed, all their transactions in the shares of companies involved in the OP.

The same disclosure obligation rests on anyone who has acquired, since the beginning of the OP, more than 0.5% of the share capital or of the voting rights at ordinary shareholders' meetings of the target company.

The COB may require any "société de bourse" to disclose the identity of a client who has given a selling order and to make a client comply with the "Réglement" of the COB.

"Offres Publique Simplifiées" (Simplified Procedure)
In certain limited cases, it is possible to use a simplified procedure subject to the approval of the CBV:

(a) OPs for 100% of the share capital and the voting rights of the target company by an offeror already holding, directly or indirectly, alone or in concert, more than 50% of the share capital and of the voting rights;
(b) offers by an offeror, acting alone or in concert, for the acquisition from one or several selling shareholders of such target company, of a block of shares which, together with the offeror's existing shareholding voting rights, represents 50% of the share capital or voting rights of the target company.
(c) offers restricted to 10% of the target company's share capital with voting rights, or for share capital and voting rights which, together with the offeror's existing shareholding (whether direct or indirect) and voting rights, represents 10% of the target company's voting rights;
(d) offers by an offeror, acting alone or in concert, for specific types of securities (e.g. for preferred shares, "certificats d'investissement" giving only an entitlement to dividends, "certificats de droit de vote" giving only an entitlement to voting rights);
(e) redemption offers with a view to cancellation of the shares for which the offer is made.

Where the offeror holds, directly or indirectly, more than 50% of the share capital and voting rights of the target company (see (a) above), the price may not be lower than the average market price, weighted by the amount of transactions, during the 60 market days preceding the publication of the "avis de dépôt" of the OP.

OPs subject to a simplified procedure must remain open for at least 10 market days in the case of an OPA for at least 15 market days in the case of an OPE, as opposed to 20 market days for OPs subject to the standard procedure.

Under the simplified procedure where a person (or persons acting in concert) proposes to acquire a block of shares representing more than 50% of the share capital or the voting rights of a quoted company (see (a) above), the purchaser may make a prior application to the CBV for authorisation to make an offer to all the shareholders to buy their shares at the same price. This offer must be maintained in being for at least 10 to 15 market days and is known as "procédure de garantie de cours".

The "procédure de garantie de cours" may also apply when the block of shares is acquired indirectly through the purchase of a holding company (whether quoted or not), the main asset of which is represented by the block of shares.

The price offered to the minority shareholders must be purchase price for the block of shares unless the CBV authorises a lower price which must be justified by the existence of a specific risk undertaken by the seller of the block or a deferred payment to the seller of the block.

When the payment is deferred, the discount rate may not be higher than the market interest rate in force at the time of the sale.

The purchaser is committed to purchase all the shares from shareholders willing to sell and may not make its commitment conditional upon a minimum percentage of shares being offered in response.

"Offres Publiques de Retrait" (OPR)

Pursuant to the Law of 2nd August 1989 (see p.71 *et seq.* minority shareholders of a company whose shares are quoted on the official market or on the second market may withdraw from the company under the following circumstances:

(a) when a person or persons acting in concert hold at least 95% of the voting rights of a company, then one or several minority shareholders may require the CBV to cause the majority shareholders too submit a public offer to purchase the shares held by the minority shareholders in such company. Upon receipt of this request, the CBV notifies the company and reviews the terms and conditions of the OPR with the company and with the financial institutions which guarantee the due performance of the transaction. Even in cases where the majority shareholders hold 95% of the voting rights in the company, the CBV may nevertheless refuse to comply with the request of the minority shareholders especially if it is of the opinion that the market in which the shares are traded is sufficiently liquid.

(b) When a person or persons acting in concert hold at least 95% of the voting rights at general meetings, one or several majority shareholders may also require the delisting of the company. In such a case, the OPR replaces the "squeeze-out" procedure which is unknown under French company law. The shares of the company are then delisted when the OPR has expired (whatever its result may be) and the company is no longer regarded as a public company. However, it should be borne in mind that the CBV or the COB may refuse the delisting of the shares (see para above).

(c) When an SA is transformed into an SCA, the majority shareholders holding at least two-thirds of the voting rights of the company must submit an OPR to purchase the shares of the minority shareholders immediately after the resolution regarding the transformation has been passed by the general meeting.

(d) When one or several controlling shareholders (e.g. the shareholders holding directly or indirectly the majority of the voting rights at general meetings or who control the company *de facto*) intend to modify significantly the company's articles of association or the company's activity, the CBV should then be notified of the proposed modification and should review with the controlling shareholders whether the implementation of an OPR or not is appropriate. A significant modification of the company's articles of association or company's activity includes, pursuant to Article 5–5–5 of the CBV "Réglement Général", the transformation of the company, the modification of the conditions for the transfer of shares, such as the insertion of an approval clause, and the transfer or contribution to another company of all or the main corporate assets.

The CBV reviews the consequences of the proposed transaction compared with the shareholders' rights and interests and sets forth, with the agreement of the controlling shareholders, the conditions of the OPR, such as the purchase price. It should be noted that the minority shareholders can validly refuse the public offer submitted by the controlling shareholders as they cannot be excluded from the company against their will.

The implementation of the OPR is subject to the same rules as those applicable to the "offre publique simplifiée" (see p.83 *et seq.*). The COB may require the offeror to draft a "note d'information" except when the offeror holds at least 95% of the voting rights of the company. In such case, the shareholders in a group of shareholders holding at least 95% of the voting rights must publish in a financial newspaper, no later than the day preceding the opening of the OPR, an announcement subject to the supervision of the COB specifying how the purchase price was determined, the intentions of the purchasers, the circumstances of the transaction and the means of finance.

"Offres Publiques de Vente" (OPV)

The owner of shares quoted on the official market or on the second market or traded over-the-counter may announce to the public its intention to sell all or part of its shares at a fixed price pursuant to an OPV procedure. The OPV is a normal method of registering new shares on the official market or on the second market. Unless otherwise stipulated by the CBV, the offer must be related to shares representing either (a) not less than 10% of the share capital of the relevant company, or (b) at least 20 times the daily trading in the market for the shares during the six months preceding the OPV.

The offeror must submit to the CBV an offer including the following information, nameley: the purpose of the transaction, the number and class of the shares subject to the OPV, the minimum number (if any) of the shares to be sold, the selling price of the shares and the terms of payment. The seller commits himself irrevocably when submitting the offer to the CBV.

Upon receipt, the CBV notifies the offer to the Treasury Department and to the COB and, if necessary, decides to suspend the quotation of the shares. If the CBV approves the offer, the SBF must then advise the public of the terms of the OPV by publishing an announcement in the "bulletin officiel de la cote". The information to be given to the public depends on the percentage number of shares offered for sale:

- When the OPV is for 15% or more of the shares, the offeror must publish in a financial newspaper an announcement, subject to the prior approval of the COB, immediately after the CBV has published its approval of the OPV. The offeror must give details in the announcement as to its purpose, how the sales price was determined, the number and characteristics of the shares the subject of the sale as well as the number of shares which the offeror intends to retain, if any.

- When the OPV is for less than 15% of the shares, the offeror must then draw up an information notice to be submitted to the COB for its prior approval and published in a financial newspaper at least three market days before the expected date of opening of the OPV. In cases where the target company does not draw up with the offeror a joint information notice, it must itself then publish an announcement, also subject to the prior approval of the COB, specifying the comments made by the board of directors or the directorate on the proposed transaction.

The offeror may increase the proposed sales price by at least 5% provided this increase occurs no later than two market days before the expected date of the opening of the OPV. If the OPV is successful, the shares are quoted at their sales price.

Protection against Hostile Takeover Bids

Protection in this particular field is tantamount to prevention, since once an OPA has been launched there is very little the target company can do, other than try to find a white knight. In particular it is not possible to implement a capital increase unless a general meeting of shareholders has been held or has been called prior to publication of the takeover bid.

Preventative measures, in France as elsewhere, involve certain well-known techniques: the creation of stable groups of shareholders ("noyaux durs"), cross-participations (which are prohibited in excess of 10%), the issue of securities convertible into shares (for example convertible bonds, bonds redeemable in shares, or bonds carrying subscription warrants for shares), the issue of shares carrying double voting rights (this is only possible where fully paid-up shares have been owned by the same shareholder for a minimum period of not less than two years but no more than four years) or the issue of shares carrying preferred dividends without voting rights and investment certificates without voting rights (neither of these categories may exceed 25% of the share capital).

A company can also validly limit in its articles of association the voting rights attributable to each shareholder, (by way of exception to the general principle that the voting rights attached to shares must be pro rata to their percentage of the share capital). This provision (resulting from the application of Article L.177 of the French Company Law) can even be inserted into the company's articles of association by an extraordinary shareholders' meeting held subsequent to the registration of the company. In the absence of statutory provisions relating thereto, the maximum number of voting rights can be freely determined within the articles of association: the maximum voting rights can correspond to a specific figure (such as 100) or can decrease pro rata to the number of shares held; such provision may be limited to specific shareholders' meetings (ordinary or extraordinary, or to meetings with a specific agenda).

Under French company law, the limitation must be imposed on all the shareholders, irrespective of the class of shares held, (except for preferred shares without voting rights).

Furthermore, provisions whereby shares held by a group of shareholders or by shareholders acting in concert are regarded as held by a single shareholder for the purpose of calculating the limitation on voting rights, should be unenforceable. Some companies whose shares are quoted on the Stock Exchange have inserted in their articles of association another type of limitation on voting rights, whereby no shareholder can exercise his voting rights beyond a maximum percentage, irrespective of his shareholding.

Although the limitation on voting rights is a deterrent to a potential raider unless he can spread out his shares among friendly individual or corporate shareholders, this preventative technique entails drawbacks for the existing controlling shareholders, who are also subject to the same restriction as the potential raider.

As explained above, some companies insert in their articles of association clauses whereby sales of shares to persons who are not already shareholders must receive the prior approval of the board of directors ("clause d'agrément") or must be subject to a right of first refusal on the part of other shareholders ("clause de préemption"). As already outlined (see p.73 *et seq.*), "clauses d'agrément" must now be withdrawn from the articles of association of companies applying for a listing and must be disclosed to the CBV and the public when they are introduced subsequently. Existing regulations do not contain any explicit prohibition on "clauses de préemption" but the position of the COB is that they must be removed or regarded as unenforceable.

Some corporate forms such as the SCA are also appropriate when implementing a preventative measure against hostile takeover bids, for the reasons set out at para above.

Finally acquisitions of shares in quoted companies must be notified to the company and to the CBV when certain percentages are reached. Thus a purchaser must inform the CBV within five days and the company within fifteen days when he holds more than 5, 10, 20, 33, 50 or 66.66% respectively of the shares. The obligation applies both to the purchaser and to other persons acting on his behalf or in concert with him. Failure to notify entails a prohibition against voting the relevant shares for a period of two years. When a person holds 20% or more of the shares of a quoted company he must declare to the COB his intentions regarding future purchases of shares and his strategy for the next 12 month period.

Criminal Violations Regarding Quoted Shares

Insider Dealing

Insider dealing is punishable by criminal and administrative penalties which can be served consecutively.

First the criminal penalties. Pursuant to Article 10–1 of sub-section 1 of the Ordinance of 28th September 1967, any insider ("initié") and any person having access in the course of his professional functions to privileged information on the prospects or position of an issuer of securities or on the prospects of a security, who, before such information was made available to the public, shall have carried out or knowingly caused to be carried out on the market either directly or indirectly one or several transactions, may be sentenced to:

- a prison term of two months to two years; and/or
- a fine of FF 6000 to FF 10m, subject to a maximum in excess of FF 10m, equal to 10 times the amount of the profit actually made by the insider, but which may in no case be lower than such profit.

Pursuant to the Ordinance of 28th September 1967, insiders may comprise and include all categories of persons subject to the supervision of the COB under Article L.162–1 of the French Company Law, i.e.:

- the president, the directors and the general managers of an SA in the traditional form;
- the members of the directorate or supervisory board of an SA in the double-tier form;
- the "Gérant" and members of the supervisory board of an SCA;
- the spouses of the above-mentioned categories of persons.

It should be noted that in addition to these categories which are addressed by French company law, any person having access through his professional functions to privileged information, (e.g. *de facto* insiders) even though such person is not employed by the company, is considered as a potential offender. When the insider is a legal entity its officers, whether *de jure* or *de facto*, are liable for criminal offences committed by the legal entity.

Consequently an obligation to abstain from trading is imposed on any person who is aware of specific information not yet available to the public which may have a bearing on the price of security.

The privileged information referred to in the Ordinance of 28th September 1967 must be "precise, particular and certain" and such privileged information may have been obtained by a material fact (even fortuitous) or through confidential information whenever it is related to the technical, commercial or financial operation of a company and whenever it is obtained in the course of professional activity.

The criminal offence may also result from purchase or sale orders traded on foreign Stock Exchanges whenever such orders were given from France.

The obligation to abstain from trading is reinforced by an obligation of confidentiality vis-à-vis third parties unaware of such information; in fact any person having access in the course of his professional activities and/or of his functions to privileged information who discloses such information to a third party outside the normal course of his activities may also be sentenced to a prison term of between one to six months and/or to a fine of between FF 10,000 to FF 100,000.

The insider must not necessarily have fraudulent or speculative intention. It is sufficient if he acted or caused another to act with the knowledge that such information was not yet available to the public.

In addition to criminal penalties there are administrative penalties. Regulation 90–08 of the COB provides for prohibitions regarding the use, (whether for their own account or for the account of third parties) and the dissemination of privileged information by the following persons:

- the holders of privileged information by virtue of their functions in the company (e.g. members of the board of directors, supervisory board or management board or persons carrying out any other official functions in the company) (the internal primary insiders);
- the holders of privileged information as a result of the preparation or completion of a financial transaction (external primary insiders);
- the holders of privileged information as a result of direct or indirect disclosure of such information made to them by the above-mentioned categories of persons provided they were aware of the privileged nature of such information and they knew such information was given from a primary or secondary insider (external third insiders). The prohibition against dissemination of privileged information does not apply to this last category of insiders.

When the above prohibitions are infringed, the COB can sentence the offenders to a fine of an amount up to FF 10m.

False or Misleading Information

Pursuant to Article 10–1, subparagraph 3 of the Ordinance of 28th September 1967, any person who knowingly circulates to the public by any means false or misleading information on the prospect or position of an issuer of securities or on the prospects of a security, such as to influence the quotation of such security, is punishable by the same criminal penalties as those applicable to the use of privileged information.

Furthermore, the wilful dissemination to the public of any inaccurate, untrue or misleading information regarding the issuer of the securities or the securities themselves, is regarded as a breach of the obligation to ensure that the public is well and properly informed. Any person responsible for such dissemination may be subject to fines.

Influencing the Price of a Security
Any person who wilfully carries out (whether directly or indirectly) or attempts to carry out on the market where a security is quoted an act intended to influence the normal operation of the market by deceiving another party may be subject to a prison term of two months to two years and/or to a fine of FF 6,000 to FF 10m, it being understood that this maximum amount may reach 10 times the profit actually made. Article 10–3 of the Ordinance of 28th September 1967 deals specifically with this offence.

V. TAX CONSIDERATIONS

General Overview

Corporate Income Tax

Under the territoriality principle, industrial and commercial profits generated by a commercial company or by an individual carrying on industrial and commercial activities are liable for French tax if earned in France or if taxation of such profits is permitted under a tax treaty. This principle is subject to exceptions such as the worldwide taxation of income (e.g. when French companies have been permitted by the Ministry of Economy and Finance to be taxed on their worldwide income or to compute their taxable profits by adding to their French source profits the profits of the French or foreign companies in which they directly or indirectly hold at least 50% of the voting rights).

Corporate income tax is imposed on the income received by SAs, SCAs and SARLs. However, when the SARL has one shareholder who is an individual (in such case, it is called a EURL), it is not subject to corporate income tax (unless the shareholder so elects) and profits are then taxed in the hands of the individual shareholder according to his individual tax regime.

SNCs, GIEs and "sociétés en participation" are excluded from the scope of corporate income tax unless they exercise an option for liability to corporate tax. These partnerships are considered to have fiscal transparency for French tax purposes, i.e. each of the partners is subject to taxation on the portion of the income which he derives from the company according to his individual tax regime.

Profits attributable to the "commandités" of an SCS are taxed in their hands, whereas the portion of profits attributable to the "commanditaires" is always subject to corporate income tax at the company's level.

French branches of foreign companies are liable for corporate income tax as the French tax principle is that earnings from an establishment operated in France are subject to corporate tax in France. Furthermore, a French branch of a foreign company will be subject to a 25% withholding tax on its after tax profit deemed to be distributed, unless a tax treaty reduces this withholding tax or unless it can be proved that no distribution of dividends occurred.

Apart from corporate tax, there is an annual minimum company tax which is due from all entities subject to the payment of corporate income tax. This tax varies from FF 5000 to FF 100,000 depending on turnover of the entity concerned (FF 100,000 being applicable to entities whose turnover exceeds FF 500m) and is due irrespective of the profit or loss position of the company concerned.

Tax Losses Rules

Tax Losses Carry-forward

Ordinary losses incurred during a tax year may be carried forward for five years and may be used to set off against income of the first available year during the five-year carry-forward period. As an exception to this rule, losses resulting from depreciation may be carried forward indefinitely ("amortissements réputés différés").

The following limitations apply to losses carried forward in the context of mergers:

(a) The losses of the absorbed company generated before the effective date of the merger cannot be transferred to the absorbing company unless a special authorisation is granted by the Ministry of Economy and Finance. It should be borne in mind that the authorities have total discretion to grant or refuse such such a tax benefit.

(b) Furthermore, in the context of a merger or spin-off (representing more than 5% of the business of the company), the depreciation indefinitely carried forward ("amortissements réputés différés") in both companies become ordinary losses (i.e. losses carried forward over a five-year period) unless a special authorisation is granted by the Ministry of Economy and Finance. However, the computation of the five-year period starts as from the date of creation of the "amortissements réputés différés".

Tax Losses Carry-back

Companies may also carry back losses incurred in the financial year of the election against the undistributed profits of the last three financial years. The deficit is first set off against the undistributed income of the first available year. The excess tax income deemed to have been paid after carrying back losses will be available as a tax credit against payment of corporate income tax due over the subsequent five years and will be reimbursed after this period if not allocated to the payment of the corporate income tax.

Business Capital Gains

Capital gains realised by companies are subject to taxation as follows:

- the net short-term capital gains made on assets which have been held for less than two years before disposal are subject to tax at the standard corporate income tax rate; depreciation recaptures are always regarded as short-term capital gains, notwithstanding the date of acquisition of the asset sold;
- the net long-term capital gains are taxed at the rate of 18%, except for long-term capital gains on certain portfolio securities (such as bonds, interests in mutual funds and SICAVs) which are taxed at the standard corporate income tax rate.

For the taxation of long and short-term capital gains, gains and losses are offset against each other and only the excess of gains over losses is subject to tax. However, it is not possible to use long-term capital losses to offset short-term capital gains or normal trading profits.

Taxation of Dividends

At the Level of the Distributing Company

If the French company makes distributions out of earnings which have not been subject to the full French corporate tax rate or which are more than five years old, the French company will have to make a payment to the French Treasury ("précompte") equal to the tax credit ("avoir fiscal") corresponding to such distribution.

Distributions of dividends made to a shareholder domiciled outside France are subject to a 25% withholding tax, which is normally reduced to 5% or 15% when a tax treaty applies.

At the Level of the Recipient Company

A French holding company receiving dividends from a French subsidiary is entitled to a tax credit ("avoir fiscal") equal to 50% of the dividends received. This tax credit constitutes, together with dividends received, a taxable income at the level of the French holding company. The "avoir fiscal" aims to diminish double taxation resulting from taxation both at the company level and at the shareholder level as follows.

Assume a corporate shareholder receives a net dividend payment of 100 carrying an "avoir fiscal" of 50. If the corporate income tax rate imposed upon this shareholder is 33.33%, it will be assessed on 100 + 50 and this would result in a gross tax liability of 50 and in an actual tax due of 0 (i./e. 50-50). The tax credit is not refunded and cannot be carried forward from year to year when a company does not have sufficient income tax liability to set off in a given year in which the "avoir fiscal" becomes available. Foreign shareholders are not in principle entitled to benefit from the "avoir fiscal" unless they are so authorised under various tax treaties entered into between France and other countries.

When a French holding company subject to corporate income tax, a branch or a permanent establishment of a foreign company in France owns at least 10% of the shares of another French or foreign company, or owns shares which have a cost price of over FF 150m, the dividends (and corresponding "avoir fiscal") received from the subsidiary are then exempt from corporate income tax in the hands of the parent company under the affiliation privilege. As a consequence of this exemption, the "avoir fiscal" attached to this dividend cannot be deducted from the corporate income tax due from the parent company.

Nevertheless, when the French holding company distributes dividends to its shareholders, the corresponding "avoir fiscal" attached to the dividends can be used to avoid payment of the "précompte" normally due by the French holding company, since the dividends were exempt from corporate income tax.

When the "précompte" is payable as a result of a dividend distribution made to foreign shareholders, it will normally be refunded, after deducting the withholding tax, to the foreign dividend recipient who is not eligible for the "avoir fiscal", when there is a tax treaty between France and the country of residence of the dividend recipient.

Taxation of Interest on Inter-company Loans

Interest paid by a company to its shareholders on loans or advances from the shareholders are tax deductible subject to the following limitations:

- the share capital of the subsidiary must be fully paid up;
- if the interest rate exceeds the yearly average of gross interest paid on bonds issued by private companies (8.86% for 1992), the excess interest payment will not be deductible;
- if the "managing shareholders", i.e. the shareholders having *de jure* or *de facto* control over the subsidiary when running the subsidiary (directly or indirectly) on a day-to-day basis or owning more than 50% of its share capital, have made loans or advances totalling over 150% of the share capital, the interest expense attributable to loans or advances beyond this threshold will not be tax deductible (unless the loans or advances are granted by a French parent company eligible for the affiliation privilege as set out in p.97 *et seq.*).

Interest payments made abroad by French legal entities are exempt from withholding tax provided there is a real loan (i.e. a written contract existing prior to the payment of the principal amount with a specific maturity date and interest rate). In all other cases (including a current account agreement, which is not considered as a loan unless it satisfies the above-mentioned conditions), a withholding tax applies at the standard rate or at a lower rate where a tax treaty provides otherwise.

Tax Consolidation ("Intégration Fiscale")

Since the 1988 Finance Law, a tax consolidation regime is applicable, without requiring prior approval from the Ministry of Economy and Finance, under certain conditions, which are discussed below.

Qualifying Conditions and Tax Consolidation Parameters
Any French holding company subject to French corporate income tax under standard rules, whose share capital is not held at least as to 95% directly or indirectly by another company subject to French corporate income tax, may elect to become the sole taxpayer liable to corporate tax due on the consolidated results of the group existing between the French holding company and those of its French subsidiaries in which it holds at least 95% of the voting rights and share capital (the tax consolidation perimeter).

It is not possible to include within the tax consolidation regime a subsidiary held by another subsidiary which itself is not a group member, even if all conditions for its inclusion are met. A tax-consolidated group may only include French companies subject to French corporate tax at the full standard corporate income tax rate. Members of a group must close their financial years on the same date.

In order to benefit from this tax regime, a foreign company holding directly or indirectly French subsidiaries may either set up a French holding company or register its shares on the balance sheet of a permanent establishment in France considered to be the parent company and liable for all the tax obligations of the French group. The French holding company must have elected for this tax regime for a minimum five-year period.

Determination of the Group Taxable Result

The group taxable result is determined by the French holding company. A group result corresponds to the algebraic sum of the results of each of the tax-consolidated companies, as previously determined and declared according to ordinary rules as if they were separate taxpayers. In particular, each company determines its own net long-term capital gains or losses.

Any losses incurred by each company before the application of the tax-consolidation regime is only deductible from its own subsequent profits (tax loss carry-forward against profits/ capital loss carry-forward against long-term capital gain). However, this should not be considered as a disadvantage since the situation would be the same if the option for the tax-consolidated regime had not been exercised.

The consolidated tax result determined by the holding company is the sum of the taxable results of each group member subject to the following adjustments:

(a) Any double taxation or double deduction disappears. Therefore, any reserve for bad debts booked on receivables held by a tax-consolidated company vis-à-vis another tax-consolidated company must be added back into the group result. Similarly, any depreciation for shares booked by the holding company vis-à-vis its tax-consolidated subsidiaries must also be added back into the group result.

(b) Forgiveness of debts and direct or indirect subsidies granted between companies of the group are not taken into account in determining the group result. The 1992 Finance Law has provided that any indirect subsidy must be identified and neutralised whenever a fixed asset of a tax-consolidated company is transferred to another tax-consolidated company at a price which is different from its market value. However, this rule does not apply when the assets transferred are portfolio shares excluded from the long-term capital gains regime.

(c) Capital gains or losses resulting from the sale of assets between group members are excluded when determining the group taxable result for the financial year in which the sale took place.

(d) When shares in a company which becomes a member of the tax-consolidated group are acquired from the group's direct or indirect shareholders, a portion of the group's overall financial charges is added back to the group's taxable result. This provision even applies if the acquiring company does not borrow funds to finance the acquisition of the shares (the so-called "Charasse" amendment).

This restriction does not apply when the shares are acquired from a third party or from the group's direct or indirect shareholders if it can be proved that the group's shareholders have themselves acquired the shares from an unrelated party with the sole intention of reselling them immediately to the company.

Impact of a Tax-consolidated Company Leaving the Group

When a company ceases for any reason whatsoever to be a member of the group, there are certain adverse tax consequences. The departing company cannot carry forward the losses incurred while it was a member of the group against profits generated after its departure. These losses are definitively transferred to the group.

Any subsidy resulting from the difference between the transfer price of an asset and its real market value must be added back to the group result of the year when the company benefiting from such transaction leaves the group. The previous capital gains or losses on intra-group sales of assets are added back.

Pursuant to the 1992 Finance Law, any other subsidies and

forgiveness of debts must be added back to the group result for the year in which the company benefiting from this transaction leaves the group, but only to the extent they have been deducted from the group result of one of the five preceding years. No recapture is necessary after this five-year period.

Payment of Group Tax Liability

When electing for the tax consolidation regime, the holding company becomes the sole taxpayer of the group although each member of the group remains jointly and severally liable for the payment of the tax due (for the portion it would have paid in the absence of tax consolidation) should the holding company be in default.

The 1992 Finance Law allows the holding company to set off, against the corporate income tax due in respect of the overall group result, the aggregate annual minimum corporate tax of all the group members (see p.94 *et seq.* above), even if some of the members generate net tax losses.

Taxation of Real Estate Owned by a Company

Real estate (other than property used for industrial, commercial or agricultural purposes) – owned directly or indirectly by French or foreign companies results in the payment by the owner of an annual tax of 3% assessed on the fair market value of such real estate, subject to the following exemptions:

- if the real estate represents less than 50% of the French assets of the owner;
- if the foreign owner of such real estate is located in a country which has concluded a tax treaty with France providing for mutual administrative assistance when the foreign owner files a special return every year;
- if the company has its effective management in France or if the foreign owner is located in a country which has concluded a tax treaty with France providing for non-discrimination and if the company files a special return

every year giving information on the real property and on the company's shareholders;
- if the company's shares are quoted on the official market or on the second market of a French or foreign Stock Exchange.

The assets include French real estate or shares in a real estate company.

It should be noted that the annual tax of 3% is due in addition to the taxation of the income generated by the real property and is not deductible for tax purposes from such income.

Tax Treatment of Mergers and Acquisitions

Asset Acquisition

Taxation of the Sale of a "Fonds de Commerce"
The sale of a "fonds de commerce" is subject to transfer tax ("droit de mutation") at the rate of 14.2% on the higher of:

- the purchase price of the tangible and intangible assets transferred; or
- the fair market value of the tangible and intangible assets transferred (French General Tax Code, Article 719).

The transfer tax (deductible for tax purposes) is reduced to 7% on any amount between FF 150,000 and FF 700,000 and is reduced to nil on any amount below FF 150,000. The sale of inventories is only subject to VAT.

If the sale of a "fonds de commerce" entails the conveyancing of a commercial building, the purchaser must then pay a registration tax at the rate of approximately 18.2% of the purchase price of the real property or on its real market value if this is higher than the purchase price.

The capital gain (if any) realised by the seller is taxable under the special regime for business gains: short-term gains (i.e. where the assets were purchased or created less than two years prior to the sale or up to the amount of the depreciation previously deducted from the taxable profits) are taxed at the standard company tax rate (i.e. presently 33.33%) or according to his individual taxation rate when the seller is an individual; long-term capital gains (i.e. capital gains realised on assets which were purchased or created for more than two years) for the amount exceeding the depreciation of the assets are taxed at the rate of 18% for companies subject to corporate income tax and at the rate of 19.4% for individuals or for companies which are not subject to corporate income tax.

Taxation of Mergers

A "fusion" (merger) or "scission" (spin-off) implies the winding-up of the absorbed company and a contribution-in-kind to the absorbing company. The application of general tax rules to these transactions entails a tax burden on each company which would make their implementation extremely unattractive. The importance of merger transactions for the national economy has led to the enactment of more favourable tax rules in relation to "fusions". For the same reason, the "apport partiel d'actif" also benefits from special tax rules similar to those applicable to "fusions". Under these special tax rules, the transaction is treated as if no change had occurred regarding the business transferred and the absorbing company is deemed to conduct the business of the absorbed company in lieu of the latter without any break. These special rules only apply to companies subject to corporation tax. Where the absorbing company is a foreign company, the benefit of these special rules is subject to obtaining a prior authorisation ("agrément") from the French Ministry of Economy and Finance. These special rules provide for exemptions in the field of company tax, personal income tax, registration duty and value added tax.

Corporation Tax

Both "fusion" and "scission" imply the winding up of the absorbed or contributing company. The latter should accordingly be subject to corporation tax on the profits of its current fiscal year, and those relating to previous fiscal years whose taxation has been deferred as well as on capital gains resulting from the transaction. However under the special tax rules applicable only to the "fusion", the contribution may be exempt from capital gains tax related to both moveable and non-moveable assets and the absorbed company will only be taxed on the profits relating to its current fiscal year and on any provisions which are no longer justified. The benefit of these special rules is conditional upon the absorbing company making a number of commitments. It must:

- add back over a maximum five-year period (or 15-year period in relation to buildings) into its taxable profits all capital gains on depreciable assets;
- calculate the capital gain relating to the resale of non-depreciable assets by reference to the value they had in the accounts of the absorbed company;
- enter in its accounts the provisions and the long-term capital gains reserves of the absorbed company.

Where the transaction is a "scission" or an "apport partiel d'actif", the benefit of the special tax rules is subject to an approval given by the French Ministry of Economy and Finance. However the approval is not required for an "apport partiel d'actif" regarding a "branche compléte d'activité" (i.e. assets able to be organised as a business which can work on its own) provided the contributing company undertakes, in the "apport partiel d'actif" agreement, (a) to retain for a period of five years the shares of the receiving company renumerating the contribution, and (b) to calculate the capital gain relating to the resale of the shares of the receiving company by reference to the value of the contribution in the accounts of the contributing company.

When an "apport partiel d'actif" is placed under the common regime it must be considered as a sale of assets taxable under the regime of business gains such as referred to above. Although this common regime is not frequently applicable, an "apport partiel d'actif" may be placed under this regime when the contributing company has large tax losses carried forward which may offset the capital gains which it will make under the contribution or when the contributing company wants to sell the shares received in exchange for its contribution immediately after the contribution. Another advantage of the common regime lies in the fact that the receiving company will benefit from an upgraded basis for depreciation.

Personal Income Tax

The allotment of shares of the absorbing company to the shareholders of the absorbed company is not, under the special rules, regarded as taxable income. However the benefit of this rule is subject to obtaining an approval from the French Ministry of Economy and Finance where the transaction is a "scission", and to completion of the allotment of shares within one year from the contribution where the transaction is an "apport partiel d'actif". Such allotment is rarely made in practice since the contributing company has generally undertaken to keep the shares of the receiving company for a period of five years with a view to benefiting from the special rules relating to corporation tax.

Furthermore, the capital gains resulting for the shareholders of the contributing company from the exchange of shares are taxed at the rate of 19.4% (i.e. 16% plus extra taxes) when the shareholder is an individual and at the rate of 18% when the shareholder is a company subject to corporate income tax provided the capital gains are long term. However, this taxation may be deferred, upon request, until the time the shares allotted by the absorbing company are sold.

Registration Duty

A 1.20% duty is payable on the merger surplus, namely the difference between the net asset value of the absorbed company and the amount of its issued share capital. However, payment of this duty appears to be in contradiction with the EC Directive. Where the transaction is a "scission", the 1.20% duty is levied only if the "scission" has obtained the approval of the French Ministry of Economy and Finance.

The assumption by the absorbing company of the liabilities of the absorbed company is not subject to registration duty.

Where the contribution is an "apport partiel d'actif" of a complete and autonomous branch of activity ("branche compléte et autonome d'activité"), it may be subject to the favourable tax regime set about in Article 817 of the General Tax Code which limits the registration tax to a flat rate duty which is currently FF 1120. No prior approval of the French Ministry of Economy and Finance is required for a contribution related to a complete and autonomous branch of activity.

This favourable tax regime related to registration tax is entirely independent from the tax regime related to corporation tax (see para above). It is therefore possible to place the contribution within the favourable tax regime from a registration duty viewpoint, whereas the contribution comes under the normal regime from a company tax viewpoint.

The contribution of real property under a "fusion" or contribution of a "branche compléte et autonome d'activité" is exempt from any registration tax.

However, the advantages deriving from the favourable tax regime from a registration duty viewpoint have decreased since 1992 as a contribution of assets against shares between companies subject to corporate income tax gives rise to a flat rate registration duty of FF 500.

Value Added Tax (VAT)
The absorbed company may transfer its VAT credit to the absorbing company provided the latter undertakes to make the regularisations which were required from the absorbed company.

Share Acquisition

Taxation of Sale of Shares
A sale of shares evidenced by a written deed (which is mandatory for the transfer of shares in a SARL, SNC and SCS) is subject to a registration tax of 4.80% of the purchase price, whereas a sale of shares in an SA or SCA is subject to a registration tax of 1% of the purchase price, with a maximum limit of FF 20,000 per sale when the transfer is recorded in a document containing the identity of the parties and the purchase price. When no document in writing is produced, the sale of shares of an SA or SCA which occurs when the transfer is made from one account to the other is not subject to registration tax.

When the shares are quoted on the Stock Exchange, the sale is subject to a transfer tax ("impôt de bourse") at a proportional rate of 3 per thousand on the portion of the sale price up to FF 1 m and 1.5 per thousand above this limit with an exemption for transactions below or equal to FF 50,000. The "impôt de bourse" is tax deductible for corporate income tax.

It results from the above tax rules that a share acquisition is subject to a more favourable tax treatment in France — especially for the transfer of shares in an SA or in an SCA — than an asset acquisition (see p.104 *et seq.*).

Furthermore, as previously mentioned (see p.57 *et seq.*), the risk that the French tax authorities may disqualify the sale of 100% of the shares of a company at one time or within a short period as a sale of a business, resulting in a taxation of

14.20%, has recently disappeared.

Taxation of the Sale of Shares Held in Real Estate Companies. When a real estate company owns real property, other than for its own industrial, commercial or agricultural purposes, representing more than 50% of the value of the total corporate assets, the transfer of shares in such real estate companies (provided the shares are not quoted on the Stock Exchange) is considered for tax purposes as a transfer of real property and is accordingly subject to the same taxation, with respect to the capital gains resulting from the sale of the shares, as for the sale of real property.

VI. LABOUR LAW ENVIRONMENT

This section does not cover the issue of the prior consultation of the "Comité d'Entreprise" in the context of merger and acquisition transactions as it has been dealt with in p.36 *et seq.*.

Transfer of Employment Contracts under Merger and Acquisition Transactions

Conditions for the Application of Article L–122–12 of the French Labour Code

Pursuant to Article L–122–12 of the French Labour Code, any modification of the employer's legal position, whether as a result of a succession, sale, merger, change of the business or contribution, does not in principle affect the survival of the existing employment contracts under the same terms and conditions between the new employer and the company's employees.

Article L–122–12 can thus apply to:

- the sale of a "fonds de commerce";
- a merger or spin-off of a branch of activity;
- the acquisition of a majority shareholding;
- the absorption by a client of the activity initially performed by an outside supplier.

However, French courts require the transfer of an economic entity maintaining its identity in order to apply the provisions of Article L–122–12.

Thus, the "Cour de Cassation" has held that some drivers who were employed to transport the goods of a company, and who were subsequently transferred to an outside contractor under a transportation of goods agreement, did not maintain their employment with the same economic entity since the new outside contractor used the drivers for tasks other than those for which they were initially hired.

Consequences of the Application of Article L–122–12 of the French Labour Code

The new employer, who is regarded for legal purposes as the successor of the former employer, must take over all the employment obligations towards the employees of the business he is continuing to operate as a result of the transfer, since the underlying principle is the continuity of the existing employment contracts under the same terms and conditions.

The automatic application of article L–122–12 is difficult to circumvent since the former employer is not authorised to dismiss employees in anticipation of selling the business or to agree with the potential purchaser upon such dismissals in the course of the negotiations except (a) when the former employer can prove that the reorganisation of the business is necessary for its survival, and (b) provided there is no fraud. Fraud is established where the sole purpose of the dismissal is to deprive employees of the legal protection of Article L–122–12. The same restriction applies to the new employer if he intends to dismiss employees whose employment contracts were taken over in the course of the acquisition process.

This protected status for the employees transferred to a successor should be borne in mind in the context of negotiations for the acquisition of a business in France as no modification of the existing employment contract can be imposed by the new employer. However, prior to or following the acquisition of a business, the dismissal of employees is permitted when the appropriate economic or technical reasons required for a reduction of employees are met (see para).

Existing collective bargaining agreements ("conventions collectives") are not imposed on new employers in cases where such employers are not in the same scope of activity, as it was held by French courts that the provisions of Article L–122–12 do not apply to employees' rights resulting from collective bargaining agreements. However, most collective bargaining agreements expressly provide that the existing benefits acquired by the employees should be maintained in the event of any modification in the legal position of the employer.

In order to remedy these consequences, Article L.132–8 of the French Labour Code provides that if the application of a collective bargaining agreement in a company is challenged, especially as a result of a merger or spin-off:

- the existing collective agreement continues to apply until the collective agreement replacing the existing one comes into force or, in the absence of replacement, for a period of one-year or for such longer period as may otherwise be provided for;
- in the absence of replacement of the existing collective agreement as referred to above, the existing benefits acquired by the employees under the prior agreement must be maintained;
- furthermore, negotiations must be conducted at the re-

quest of a party in the company in order (a) either to establish a new collective agreement or (b) to adjust the status of the employees to the provisions of the collective agreement applicable to the new employer.

Collective Dismissals of Employees

Various Grounds for Employees' Dismissals

Under French labour law, employees who enjoy an employment contract with an indefinite term enjoy a protected status and cannot really be dismissed unless the dismissal is based on a real and serious cause or on economic reasons.

Dismissal for real and serious cause, i.e. when performance or qualifications are insufficient or when there is a fault committed by such employee, does not imply the elimination of the employee's position, whereas the position itself is eliminated when the dismissal is for economic reasons. Dismissal for economic reasons can be individual or collective but only collective dismissals are discussed below.

Procedure for Collective Dismissals for Economic Reasons (Redundancies)

Redundancies are regulated by Law No. 89–459 of 2nd August 1989 which has significantly amended the French Labour Code designed to reduce the number of employees being made redundant. Since the coming into force of the Law of 2nd August 1989, Article L–321–1 of the Labour Code gives the following definition of a redundancy ("licenciement pour motif économique") made by an employer. It is a redundancy if the dismissal is made:

- for one or more reasons unconnected with the person being made redundant; and
- resulting from the elimination or transformation of the position or from a substantial modification of the employ-

ment contract arising from economic difficulties or technological changes.

It follows from the new statutory definition that when an employee refuses to accept a substantial modification of his employment contract resulting from economic difficulties or technological changes, such employee shall then be considered to have been made redundant.

In addition to the obligation to comply strictly with the redundancy procedure, the employer incurs an obligation to use its best efforts to find alternative placement opportunities ("obligation de recherche de possibilités de reclassement") which has a broad scope: although this obligation is only set out explicitly in a provision of the French Labour Code governing redundancies of 10 or more employees, court decisions have held that it is a general obligation incurred by any employer carrying out redundancies, whether individual or collective.

The procedure, the main steps of which are described below, should be strictly complied with by the employer, as any failure to respect (*inter alia*) the statutory deadline would render the redundancy irregular and would result in damages.

Redundancies of Two to Nine Employees

The regulations regarding this type of collective redundancy of less than 10 employees over a 30 day period is more flexible than when 10 or more employees are made redundant. Under such circumstances, no social plan is required but a mere post-redundancy notification must be sent to the labour authorities.

Successive redundancies of less than 10 employees in the same company would result in the application of the regulations for large redundancies of 10 or more employees (see p.116 *et seq.*).

The main steps of the applicable standard procedure are as

follows (a special procedure applies to the redundancy of protected employees who are the employees' representatives and the trade union representatives):

- establishing the order of the redundancies of the employees, together with the criteria established in deciding such order, bearing in mind that the employer is free to establish the order according to the criteria he thinks most appropriate; however, the employer must respond to the employees' request, if any, regarding the criteria used for the order of the redundancies;
- establishing with the social security authorities a reconversion contract which aims at assisting the employees in finding a new qualification;
- convening the employees' representatives (workers' council or employees' delegates in companies with less than 50 employees) and consulting the employees' representatives on the redundancy proposal and on the employees reconversion contract;
- calling each employee who is to be made redundant to a preliminary meeting; this convening must be made by registered letter and must indicate the purpose of the meeting, the date, the time and place of the meeting; the employee can be assisted by a representative of his choice (such as an employee's representative, any employee of the company or an outside advisor);
- holding a preliminary meeting with each employee: this individual meeting (where the employer must also propose a reconversion contract) will be followed by the sending of the redundancy letter to the relevant employee unless the employee accepts the reconversion contract within a special statutory deadline;
- notifying the local labour authorities (Director of Labour in the Department) of the redundancies made (including the comments of the employees' representatives);
- complying with the preemptive right to be rehired. In

fact, pursuant to the Law of 2nd August 1989, the employees made redundant have a preemptive right to be reemployed in the company that made them redundant. When advised by the employees of their intention to exercise their right to be rehired, the employer must, for a period of one year following the termination of their respective employment contracts, notify those employees of any job which could match their qualifications. This obligation of the employer must be taken seriously, since failure to comply with it would result in damages equal to at least two months' salary.

Redundancies of 10 or More Employees

The redundancy of 10 or more employees over a 30 day period is similar to the procedure set out above, but the employer is also obliged to establish a social plan, the purpose of which is to avoid redundancies or to reduce the consequences of redundancy and to assist the employees made redundant in their reconversion so far as possible. Since Law No. 93–121 of 27th January 1993, the contents of the social plan must reflect the attempts developed by the employer to procure the placement of the employees made redundant. Thus the social plan must contain some statutory provisions concerning placement (monitored by the labour authorities), namely:

- provisions as to internal placement (such as a change of job in the employing company) to be offered in priority to employees aged over 50 and to handicapped employees;
- reduction and adjustments to working time (e.g. through part-time jobs on progressive retirements);
- measures of external placement carried out by the creation of a special entity (possibly with several other companies) in charge of assisting employees with their placement and providing employees with financial incentives in certain cases;
- financial, commercial or technical assistance granted to

an employee made redundant who creates his own enterprise;
- action for training and conversion.

The drafting of the social plan should then be carefully reviewed in the light of the coming into force of the Law of 27th January 1993: the social plan must be subject to the review and comments of the labour authorities and of the employees' representatives. The labour authorities can reject the social plan if the contents, notably the provisions concerning placement, are not, in their opinion, satisfactory.

The employees' representatives must be convened at two successive meetings. The convening letters sent to the employees' representatives must include information on the proposed social plan and the social provisions proposed. Two successive meetings must be held with the employees' representatives in order to discuss the proposed redundancies, separated by a maximum of 14 to 28 days depending on the number of employees to be made redundant. The purpose of these meetings is to enable the employees' representatives to submit suggestions to the employer, who must give a response to such proposals.

Furthermore, the employees' representatives are authorised by law to require the assistance of an accountant ("expert comptable") appointed at the first meeting. In this case, three meetings of the employees' representatives must be held instead of two. The accountant should have access to the same information as the company's own "expert comptable" in order to make his report on the proposed redundancies.

The redundancy of employees aged over 50 in the context of redundancies of more than nine employees should be carefully considered. Pursuant to the Law of 27th January 1993 the labour authorities indirectly supervise the redundancies of this type of employee and they can validly reject a social plan failing to provide for serious provisions concerning the placement of this type of employee.

Redundancies Carried out during Bankruptcy Proceedings

The procedure applicable is somewhat simplified in the case of bankruptcy proceedings as there is frequently considerable urgency on making the redundancies:

- when redundancies are carried out over the observation period (i.e. the period during which a legal administrator reports on whether or not the company should be maintained), the legal administrator must notify the employees' representatives and the relevant labour authorities of the proposed redundancies and submit the redundancies to the approval of the bankruptcy judge, bearing in mind that the legal administrator must prove he used his best efforts to find new placements for the employees made redundant;
- in the context of an organisation plan submitted by the legal administrator, the employees' representatives must be consulted on the proposed redundancies and the labour authorities must be notified before the bankruptcy judge approves the redundancies;
- if the company is to be liquidated, the employees' representatives must be consulted and the labour authorities informed as to the proposed redundancies.

Reconversion contracts must be proposed to the employees to be made redundant even during the bankruptcy proceedings, it being understood that the relevant employees must elect within seven days to benefit from the reconversion contract.

Index